HOW TO SURVIVE BEING A PRESBYTERIAN!

How to Survive Being a Presbyterian!

▼

A Merry Manual Celebrating the Foibles of the Frozen Chosen

Bob Reed

Illustrations by Deborah Zemke

Writers Club Press
San Jose New York Lincoln Shanghai

How to Survive Being a Presbyterian!
A Merry Manual Celebrating the Foibles of the Frozen Chosen

Writers Club Press
an imprint of iUniverse.com, Inc.

For information address:
iUniverse.com, Inc.
5220 S 16th, Ste. 200
Lincoln, NE 68512
www.iuniverse.com

The story titled "The Four W's Rule" on pages 108-110 is an abbreviated version of the title story in *The Potluck Dinner That Went Astray—And Other Tales of Christian Life,* also by the author (Smyth & Helwys Publishers).

For all other inquiries and correspondence:
Reed-Gordon Books
285 Burr Road, East Northport, NY 11731
reedgordon@aol.com
fax and phone: (631) 462-5627

ISBN: 0-595-15225-2

Printed in the United States of America

Contents

"Angels can fly because they take
themselves lightly."
G. K. Chesterton

So it hopefully is with my
fellow Presbyterians,
to whom this book
is dedicated.

Acknowledgments

Some convivial lay people looked over this manuscript and offered suggestions and advice about additions and deletions. Among them were Chuck and Leonora Marquis, Marcia and Ron Mercer, and Charlie and Bette Carcano, Presbyterians all.

Some of the denomination's distinguished retired pastors also took a look at the piece and offered their most helpful comments. Others corrected historical and theological mistakes. All were unfailingly gracious.

Some active Presbyterian pastors including the Ministry of Laughter founder, the Reverend Doyne Michie, were most helpful. My fellow Iowan (now in New Jersey) who goes by the name of the Reverend David Harvey contributed salutary suggestions. And the Reverends Louise Armstrong and John Underwood offered their wonderfully constructive comments. My previous Methodist minister, the Reverend T. Samuel Lee, also brought a unique perspective to this effort.

Deborah Zemke caught the spirit of the piece in her truly imaginative art; Clark and Sandy Godfrey incorporated it.

All of my family contributed their professional skills and expertise to the project. My daughter Deri brought her remarkable editing talents to the process. My son Bob applied his formidable Web mastery to the marketing of the endeavor. My Emmy-award-winning son Rick will produce the forthcoming video. And my wife Max took time off and lent her own editing and formatting abilities to the work. She also applied her blessed patience.

None of the above, however, are responsible for any of the thoughts and ideas or any errors of commission or omission in this little manual. They are the author's alone.

The ideas and statements herein are those of the author and are not officially or unofficially in any way whatsoever, those of the Presbyterian Church (U.S.A.), familiarly known as the PCUSA. And this little book is void where prohibited.

Preface

This is a little book about a very special people. They are mostly WASPs, a term that others may use somewhat disparagingly today. Some wags even joke that the term originally stood for "White Anglo-Saxon PRESBYTERIANS."

The author is aware that there are many other members of our church in many other countries. And that some 7 percent of the members of the Presbyterian Church in the United States are African American, Native American, Asian American, or Hispanic. They all make up God's rainbow here on earth. Although the lack of minority members in the American church is being vigorously addressed, their current few members is not funny.

So, how does one speak for—and to—ALL Presbyterians? You can't, of course. We are all quite different and tend to agree with Emerson that "a foolish consistency is the hobgoblin of little minds." But this attempt makes a bit of a stab at some supposed constants in our denomination, all in the interest of playful fun.

For this wee offering of love is intended to be affectionately humorous. Not everything in it is true and much of it is exaggerated. And except for those historical and publicly recognized events and people, any resemblance to actual incidents or persons living or dead is purely coincidental.

This book is not a theological tome for use by professional clergy. It is an attempt to mischievously celebrate and explain the seemingly unexplainable to the layperson. It's ostensibly designed to be a sort of tongue-in-cheek *Preppy Handbook* for new members of the church or to those returning to the fold.

Our congregations need new blood and the younger members often need some orientation or reorientation about our beloved denomination. There is recent evidence that parents with young kids are finding or returning to the church. Today's new Presbyterians should be informed by—or reminded of—our past, for they are inevitably somewhat defined by it. Perhaps if they better understand our traditionally perceived image by reading this unauthorized version of *Presby 101,* they can help change some of it in an invigorating and positive way.

So this effort is based on the cheeky observations of the author and is designed to poke a bit of raffish fun at the quiet solemnity of many of our lives—acting as a sort of prickly cactus with a pink blossom. The author is also a bit aged and 13 years-new to the denomination, and it is therefore a bit presumptuous to give advice to younger folk—particularly those who are—or were—Cradle Presbyterians.

But hopefully, a gentle ribbing of our traditional image might wake us up with a little pinch to more actively pursue some of the joy and laughter that is so available in our emerging new church. Perhaps if we can have a bit of a giggle about the supposed alchemy of our denomination, it will help us to not take ourselves so seriously so much of the time.

For as one of our distinguished clergy, the Chaplain of the United States Senate—the Reverend Dr. Lloyd John Ogilvie—notes, "Joy is the missing ingredient in contemporary Christianity. The problem is our powerless piousness and grim religiosity." And it is this writer's belief that in our spiritual life, we should be pulled by joy rather than pushed by fear.

Finally, this little book might also be read with some profit by those who have no church home and a casual interest in our denomination. It is also hoped that this field guide will be read by people who have a different faith tradition and perspective, and who seek a chuckle and some basic knowledge of the traditional habitats, feeding grounds, and proclivities of a wonderful and very special people—the Presbyterians!

B.R.
East Northport
New York
2001

Calvin
Knox
VERY
FIRST
PRESBYTERIAN

Chapter One

IN THE BEGINNING

PERCY T. PRESBY'S INSIGHT INTO THE CREATION

Some Presbyterians don't believe in Darwin's Theory of Evolution, and thus maintain that when Adam and Eve were created, they were immediately issued the regulation church tie and denominational handbag.

THE LAWS AND OBSERVATIONS OF PERCY T. PRESBY

Although you will never find his name in the history books, Percy T. Presby was a patriotic Presbyterian layman in New England in the mid-1700s. He served a number of churches in Connecticut and New York as a circuit rider, traveling long distances on horseback to help the Calvinists in that section of the country. He conducted services and preached.

But there were a number of Tories in the area who were loyal to the Crown. This reportedly led to at least one dramatic confrontation between the good patriot and the people.

As the story goes, Mr. Presby was midway through his sermon one Sabbath morn when a loyal subject of the king rose and fired his flintlock at him just at the height of one of his most rhetorical flourishes. Believing the action to be a criticism of his religious message (not his politics) Percy dove behind the pulpit, clutching his sermon and hollering, "WHERE WERE YOU WHEN THE PAPER WAS BLANK?"

The BLAM! startled the birds in the rafters, who fluttered about, adding to the commotion by knocking Widow Perkins' bonnet askew. Some of the veterans of the French and Indian War dropped to the floor, some folks in the front pew scattered, and three babies set up a howl.

Order was eventually restored, but the shaken layman was understandably never quite the same in the pulpit after that. In fact, he stopped preaching entirely.

Percy did, however, pen a number of aphorisms and canards that, over the years, have codified themselves into supposed laws and observations about the denomination. Even though he looks about 50, he is now nearly 300 years old. But the venerable layman still wanders around some churches pontificating and muttering the friendly admonitions that are included in this text at various points. He attributes his longevity to his Presbyterianism, for he notes that many members of our church never stop talking long enough to die.

Percy's little quips should probably be committed to memory by every new member of our denomination and carefully studied by those interested in Presbyterian foibles. And what does the middle initial T in Percy T. Presby stand for? The.

THE TWO JOHNS

Although he is based on an historical character, Percy T. Presby is fictitious. But you may have heard something about the two real guys who were actually responsible for the creation of our denomination nearly five centuries ago—John Calvin and John Knox. They were interesting fellows.

Calvin came along in the middle of the 16th century, about 20 years after Martin Luther broke from the Roman Catholic Church and began the Protestant Reformation. Our founder was a Frenchman who studied law but got sidetracked by a traumatic experience and became a Protestant. Building on Luther's work, he continued the reform movement.

Calvin claimed to be a rather shy scholar who sought to live "at peace in some unknown corner." Instead, he was pulled into the center of the heretical movement to reform what many had come to believe was a corrupt Roman Catholic faith.

In Calvin's case, he set out to teach the church his interpretation of the Reformation and he centered his attention on the city-state of Geneva. He did so by churning out an almost unending number of treatises and commentaries. And he became so successful that he was driven out of town for three years; in exile, he revised and expanded his masterwork, *The Institutes of the Christian Religion.* It became the classic statement of Reformed theology.

Calvin was invited to return to Geneva by the city fathers and created a theocracy. He oversaw laws passed against drunkenness, adultery, debauchery, and profanity. Playing cards and even dancing in one's own home was forbidden. Worldly dress was banned. Babies' names were restricted to those in the Bible and children could be imprisoned for lying. His command of the city left him free to spread the Reformation throughout Europe.

This stern, beak-nosed intellectual evidently preached and wrote as if words were water. He appears to have had an opinion on everything.

In addition to his exhortations on sin, the sacraments, salvation, and other weighty matters, he addressed the issue of whether a man may marry his brother's widow (no) and what to do if one party in a marriage should contract elephantiasis (ugh).

The earnest, austere cleric's most controversial belief was in predestination. This was later to cause all sorts of discussions and interpretations of the doctrine in the Presbyterian denomination.

For the last 23 years of his life, Calvin suffered from severe medical problems and, true to form, wrote about them in excruciating detail. Thus, we know more about his kidney stones and other maladies than is probably wise. His friends urged him to marry so that there would be someone to take care of him, and after a long, half-hearted search, he wed a frail widow in August of 1540.

Calvin was constantly under attack by his critics, and he spent a great deal of time defending himself. His personal life became chaotic. He was also impoverished and his household, which included a number of relatives, was in disarray. A servant engaged by his friends to manage the place was eventually discovered to have been cheating for years by manipulating the household accounts.

Calvin finally succumbed to his many ills on May 27, 1564 in his 55th year. To some, the austere and prolific intellectual had become a dictatorial, ill-tempered tyrant whose rigid principles were an affront to the established order of things. To others, he was a saint. He was probably a little bit of both—a Renaissance Everyman. Few observers of the 20th-century American character, however, ignore the influence of Calvin's theology and democratic ideas on our modern life.

His most noted disciple was the Scotsman John Knox. He cranked up the zeal of the Calvinists another notch with his thundering rhetoric. Schooled in Glasgow and ordained as a Roman Catholic priest, he also rebelled and embraced the Reformation, but was taken prisoner by the French in 1547 and forced to serve as a galley slave for 19 months. He later studied under Calvin and returned to Scotland, where he helped lead the Protestant revolution in that country.

Knox was particularly incensed that women ruled much of Western civilization. There were three Catholic queens at the time—in France, England, and Scotland—and he denounced them all in his famous "The First Blast of the Trumpet Against the Monstrous Regiment of Women." Calling any kind of rule by women "repugnant to nature" and a "subversion of good order," he was a true chauvinist—like most men of his time. He was forced to eat some of his words in 1558 when the Protestant Elizabeth I became Queen of England, but he grew in insight and stature in political as well as ecclesiastical matters.

Under his influence, Scottish nationalism and Protestantism joined forces to overthrow the government in that country and in 1560, at the request of Parliament, Knox authored the "Confession of Faith and Doctrine." This became the official creed of the kingdom, and the Reformed Church of Scotland was created.

By all accounts, Knox was a formidable personage who "chewed the scenery," as they said in the theatrical circles of the time. His image is one of a long beard with a man attached to it. Many in the kirks (as the Scottish churches were known) feared his Old Testament-like wrath. But he did unbend a bit in old age and married a young girl.

Knox died in 1572. The name of the new denomination came into use during his tenure, when some Reformed church members began to label themselves—Presbyterians. They took their name from the Greek word for elder.

The two Johns were the most influential people in the history of the denomination. If Calvin was the father, Knox was the architect of Presbyterianism. In varying degrees, they called for a participatory and representative form of government in church affairs, with everyone contributing in a collegial atmosphere.

About the only thing the two Johns would recognize today in the church they started would be the continuing and wonderfully spirited dialogue over their ideas and theology. After nearly 500 years of talking, we followers are still at it, for they say that if you ask three

Presbyterians about something, you'll get five opinions—six if all three are pastors.

THE FROZEN CHOSEN

To many outsiders, we Presbyterians are distinguished by our supposed belief in predestination. Such a conviction, however, is not universal in our denomination. You may never even HEAR about it, or even discuss it during your membership. Contrary to popular belief, it has nothing to do with the immutability of fate.

But predestination is a quiet part of our faith heritage. And the doctrine is open to a great deal of interpretation. It was a basic tenet of John Calvin's theology. He averred that we are saved strictly by God's gift of grace and not by anything we humans can do or earn on our own. Predestination formed a major part of our *Westminster Confession of Faith* in 1647 that became the doctrine of belief for Presbyterians for many years; it remains in our *Book of Confessions.*

But many members of the church periodically agitated for a revision of the *Westminster.* They were especially anxious to modify chapter three, titled "Of God's Eternal Decree," which addressed the issue of predestination. This was the interpretation that God had chosen (or elected) only some people for faith. But certain folks will receive the gift (of salvation) and others will reject it, according to some of the many theological interpretations. Reformed Christians were therefore God's Chosen People.

It sorta' followed that salvation, therefore, is not something to be earned.

This was the very heart of strict Calvinism, but it seemed to encourage in believers a sort of fatalism and a *que sera sera* attitude. I mean, if you had no way to work toward your own salvation, what was the point of attending all those blasted committee meetings? At the least, it put a crimp in the missionary work of the church because it was difficult to recruit people to what seemed to some to be an uncertain future.

In the 1800s, the liberal wing of our denomination began attempts to rectify this supposed hindrance and promoted the notion that every sinner could gain salvation. It followed the decidedly American outlook that prided itself on independence and self reliance. People could be saved by their own power rather than by the grace of God.

The argument between the two thoughts was to rage for several years with Mark Twain (who was schooled in Presbyterian Sunday Schools and had a life-long involvement with the denomination) poking fun at what he called "Presbyterian Preforeordestination." And in spite of a modification of the Westminster Confession in 1903 and a new Confession in 1967, the doctrine and its many complex and subtle interpretations has never been satisfactorily resolved within our denomination. And no single interpretation is required. The doctrine is seldom even discussed these days.

We Presbyterians, however, are noted for being pretty firm, unyielding, and constant in our beliefs—whatever they may be. Many of our members don't know or care anything about predestination—some believe in it and others don't. But it has been the inspiration for some wags to combine the two characteristics and jokingly label us "The Frozen Chosen."

So if you don't set any store in the idea of predestination, fine. If you do, you probably already subscribe to the old saying that if you want God to laugh, tell Him—or Her—your plans.

PRESBYTERIAN LANGUAGE

In order to get along in the church, you are going to have to learn the lingo. There is a distinct vocabulary. To paraphrase Jeanne and Owen Wells, two scholars of the lexicon, there are certain traditional phrases, acronyms, and initials that are peculiar to Presbyterians—even to those who aren't otherwise peculiar. It's probably best you learn them.

To start with some basics, the initials *J.C.* are not usually used to denote John Calvin, but are rather a shorthand reference in some circles to our Savior. And the name of the denomination stems from the Greek word *presbyteros*, meaning elder. It occurs many times in the Old Testament and some 72 times in the New Testament, where it refers to people who are charged with teaching the faith and running the church. The concept was adopted by Calvin and Knox as an antidote to the hierarchy of the Roman Catholic church and is the basic form of representative government used in Presbyterianism.

Elders are elected by the local congregation to represent them. They occupy the highest office in the denomination. Along with the *deacons* (who are also elected and lead a program of compassion) and the ordained *ministers*, they pretty much run things in the church. Both the elders and deacons are also ordained.

Calvin, however, didn't use the handle "Presbyterian" to identify his Reformed Church, and neither did John Knox. In fact, most churches that follow Calvinistic theology in Europe are known as Reformed. Some of us joke that only the Presbyterians would think of a way to derive our name from our governance, and not from our theology.

The Presbyterian representative system of church government, however, later served as a political model for the founders of the United States, after what many in England called "The Presbyterian Rebellion." Today, the American church is known by the initials *P.C.*, which some people may confuse with personal computer and others with politically correct.

All of this comes under the rubric of *polity,* which is not the adhesive for false teeth once hawked by that old-time, big-mouthed comedian, Martha Raye. It's just a fancy word for governance, but we Presbyterians are in love with it and will use it 'til the sun again rises. And just so nothing gets out of hand, what with all of us people running things, there's the *B.O.,* which has nothing to do with the reason one should shy away from a fellow member, but is, rather, the *Book of Order.* This is not a menu, but the constitution regulating church life. Along with *Roberts Rules of Order*, it rules the elders.

You should also understand that the elders are not necessarily old—nor are they necessarily men. Some say that becoming an elder is apparently the only time some "ladies of a certain age" don't mind a seeming reference to that age. And today, young adults are ordained as elders. In their aggregate, the elders make up the *session,* which has nothing to do with a jazz concert. It's the governing body of a local congregation. There are some 11,216 of them.

Meetings of a session or any of its various committees are lessons in compassionate democracy. They have their own patterns and vocabulary. You probably shouldn't try to liven up the proceedings by observing that a *point of order* sounds like the entree in a restaurant. Nor should you get cute when someone *calls the question* by picking up an imaginary telephone and asking what happens if no one answers.

The minutes of the uplifting session meetings have a lot of *M.S.C.* notations. These do not refer to the old name for that institution of higher learning in East Lansing, Michigan, but rather stand for *moved, seconded, and carried.* Some matters that can't otherwise be resolved go on to a gaggle of elders and ministers in a geographical area called the *presbytery* (there are 171 of them), which acts as a sort of group bishop. Sometimes the papers wind up at a *synod,* the cluster of presbyteries in a region; there are 16 of them. And some find their way to the *G.A.,* which is not the sound made by a baby, but shorthand for the General Assembly.

It's the highest ruling body of the American church and is made up equally of more than 500 elected elders and ministers (called *commissioners*). It meets once a year. Some local church members (paraphrasing Mark Twain) say that this legislative body sometimes acts like a baby with a hammer. Others joke that when the G.A. is in session, Chicken Little was probably right!

The General Assembly receives *overtures* from the presbyteries, which are not preludes to a Broadway musical, but are rather carefully written petitions calling for some action. The missives are often full of beautiful language sometimes supported by suitable biblical references in much the same way that a stick is commandeered to prop up a window sash. The reaction of the G.A. to an overture is said to be sometimes directly related to the degree of obfuscation contained within it. Some folks think that if the commissioners can't understand the thing, they approve it, hoping that it won't do much harm!

If you attend one of the annual conclaves you may hear talk of *The Merger.* The phrase can be uttered reverently or sometimes used disdainfully. It has nothing to do with Wall Street, although some still perceive it as a leveraged buyout, while others view it as a hostile takeover. It simply refers to the merger of the southern and northern branches of the church, which occurred back in 1983.

You will also hear talk of *The Great Ends*. This is not a reference to large posteriors, but is short for *The Great Ends of the Church*, six theological principles that have historically guided church life, by defining why we have a church at all.

In the corridors, the commissioners will communicate by using a lot of initials and acronyms. You should probably understand that *C.E.* does not mean Chief Executive, but rather Christian Education (although many years ago, it referred to the interdenominational youth group, Christian Endeavor) and that *Y.A.D.* is not a new hip-hop rap group, but stands for Youth Advisory Delegate.

The letters *SC* are not the initials for that university in Los Angeles, but rather denote the highest continuing officer in the church—the Stated Clerk of the General Assembly. (You probably shouldn't ask if there is an Unstated Clerk.)

And *OGA* is not the sound of an old automobile horn, but simply the Office of the General Assembly. It's located in that dynamic hotbed of denominational activity and Presbyterian capital city, Louisville, Kentucky.

You should also note that *R.S.V.* is not a new recreational vehicle, but the *Revised Standard Version* of the Bible, and that *P.K.* stands for preacher's kid.

The parsons have their own lingo. Some *seek a call* at a *face to face* (a meeting where church representatives interview candidates for pastoral positions at their church) To *answer a call* does not mean that the pastors are on their way to the bathroom; rather, it's used when they accept a position. There, they will *fill the pulpit*—which does not mean that they are necessarily large in girth. If they don't have a permanent position, they often serve as a *stated supply pastor.* In this job they don't distribute paper and pencils to churches, but they do fill in for a set period of time to minister to congregations without an installed pastor. Some ministers are *Tentmakers,* which does not mean that they spend their time sewing. They are really part-time pastors who derive much of their income from other jobs. And each year, some parsons add the initials *H.R.* after their name. This has nothing to do with their prowess on the baseball diamond, but simply means that they are honorably retired.

Some of your fellow members will note that the ministers often talk about *effectual calling*. This does not mean switching from AT&T to MCI to get cheaper service, but is rather the belief that God does the work in permitting us to believe. Some of the older ones will occasionally refer to the *Theological Declaration of Barmen*, which is not the murky expression of a bartender's personal philosophy late on a Saturday night, but rather a church statement from 1934 averring that the Cross would overpower the swastika.

At breaks, you will also hear some wonderful phrases that are used to dress up some pretty common things. *Yoking* simply means two churches getting together to work on a mutual task or to share a pastor. And to *fellowship together* usually means to engage in small talk. You will discover, however, that many Fellowship Halls are actually gymnasiums.

You will also hear the two most common Presbyterian phrases many times over. One (taken from First Corinthians) admonishes us that all things should be done *decently and in order*. This has become a sorta' unofficial credo of the Presbyterian Church (U.S.A.), for our denomination is sometimes orderly to the point of blessed madness.

The other (while not biblically based) hopefully affirms that church decisions will be made and things will happen—*if the way be clear.* The phrase is sometimes uttered with an upward glance to see if the Son is visible in the skies.

There are, of course, hundreds of other linguistic and alphabet-soup delineations used by us Presbyterians. Some years ago, the aforementioned Jeanne Welles compiled a booklet of church-related acronyms. It ran 50 pages.

It's out of print now, so you're pretty much on your own. If you don't understand, ask. Your new friends will love you. We Presbyterians live to answer questions!

SOME UNANSWERED QUESTIONS

How do we as a denomination move forward? How do we progress? Many Presbyterians seek to "modernize" our church. They periodically propose changes in our *Book of Order*, for they believe it to be redundant, overlapping, and complex—and say that it now requires an English translation. Some think that our constitution should be simplified because too much inclusiveness without elimination may cause the document to implode.

Others feel threatened by any proposed changes. Let's keep things as they are. Why alter anything?

It all leads still others to define Presbyterianism as "an argument in progress." And to advise the need for prayer.

PERCY T. PRESBY'S DISCOVERY

If you rearrange the letters in the word Presbyterian, you can spell Best in Prayer.

SOME BASICS

There are two traditional attitudes in the denomination that sometimes cause new members some adjustment problems. They can be traced back to the Scottish side of our church. One relates to music, the other to money.

As a Presbyterian, you should probably give up the thought that the bagpipe sounds pretty much like a wounded duck. A devout member in some of our traditional churches should forgive the occasional assault on his eardrums and embrace the squawking sounds, somehow clinging to the hope that the droning will not boil the blood and may cure the ague. Many believe that pipers march when they play in an effort to avoid hearing themselves.

A few new members are said to have confessed to waking up in a cold sweat after a dream about being drummed out of the denomination to the din of 1,000 bagpipes and handed over to our friends, the Lake Woebegon Lutherans. And Garrison Keillor can tell you what happens then. This is a common nightmare. But you should probably always remember that a Presbyterian gentleman is one who can play the bagpipes, but doesn't.

You will also discover that we Presbyterians are normally quite parsimonious. We have gathered together for more than 200 years at different locations in the United States to attend the annual General Assembly. Local cab drivers are said to wince when our commissioners swarm into town because, as they tell it, the Presbyterians come armed with the Ten Commandments and a ten-dollar bill and don't break either one. Bless our Scottish roots!

ON THE TRAIL OF A CONSPIRACY OF ACCENTS

If you go to Scotland to trace your Presbyterian roots, you are bound to run into a bunch of church members who talk funny. They will have a charming, lilting accent with a lot of burring in their speech, which makes them difficult to understand. You must resist the temptation to test the old rumor that if you wake one of them up in the middle of the night, he'll talk just like the rest of us.

PERCY T. PRESBY'S LAW #1

The farther away the individual member is from the General Assembly, the more he thinks everything is under control.

OUR COMMON HUMANITY

Even if you are not an elected commissioner, you can attend a General Assembly meeting as an observer. You will find yourself blessed and inspired. Here in one place are hundreds of folks who think and act and talk and worship like—and with—you.

Well, not all of them, perhaps. For there is a wide variety of beliefs, ideas, concerns, and interests in our denomination. We are sometimes agonizingly diverse, but in that diversity is our strength.

There IS a sort of messy openness in the Presbyterian Church (U.S.A.). During the eight-day event you will discover an exhilarating hodgepodge of lunches, dinners, meetings, and booths in the exhibition hall—each touting its own agenda as a part of our denomination. There's the Witherspoon Society, the Coalition, the Covenant meetings, the Presbyterian Pro-Life luncheon, the *Outlook* dinner, the National Cross Caucus Reception, the Presbyterian Media Mission gathering, the Sophia breakfast, the Network of Presbyterian Women in Leadership, the Company of Pastors get-togethers, the OneByOne meetings, and the Presbyterian Writers Guild bash, where an annual award is presented.

There will be inspiring worship services and massed choirs that will extend a final note so far that it will almost reach heaven. There will be other—often exotic—musical numbers by ethnic groups, which enrich the soul and remind us of the internationality of our denomination. And there is a shared and wonderful fellowship and smiling camaraderie among the people in attendance.

Now, it does sometimes seem to some folk that this effort to embrace all of the religious vocabulary of the day goes a bit too far. They say that there is a growing tendency to belabor the trivial and neglect the consequential. And that some of the lively groups sometimes seem to be about two sandwiches shy of a church picnic.

But in our endeavor to be an all-inclusive denomination, we generally strive for the spiritual expansion of our thoughts and interests. Most members welcome the knocking down of barriers to a more enlightened spirituality. And to an encompassing, all-embracing potpourri of concerns and beliefs.

So if you have a chance to attend the G.A., go see for yourself. It's wonderful! Percy T. Presby says that you may even get to see some extraordinary sights such as a Tuba Choir from Cuba and an Intuit Marching Band from Anchorage playing "Onward Christian Soldiers."

PERCY T. PRESBY'S MUSINGS ON STATISTICS

A recent Gallup poll found that there are more Americans (3.7 million) who believe that they have been abducted by aliens than there are Presbyterians (2.5 million), so somebody suggested that the General Assembly appoint a committee to study the aliens' methods.

SCANDALS

You will occasionally hear some rumors to the effect that there are some nefarious goings-on in the Presbyterian Church. The recent publicity about a study on sex and the so-called Fidelity and Chastity Amendment to the *Book of Order* has led some to think that licentiousness abounds in our denomination. Not true. As many people observe, we Calvinists study sex, we don't practice it much. Similarly, the occasional gossip about possible financial rip-offs and some heavy drinking among our lively members has no actual basis in fact.

Well, maybe there was a bit of chicanery in the early days in Scotland, what with that hearsay about a few missing coppers from a pew rental account. Some of the high spirited male members of the early church in the American South were said to have pulled a cork just a little bit at barn-raisings, and evidently some others in Minnesota didn't decline an occasional invitation to hoist a coupla' beers—just to keep out the wintry night air. They joke that some of their saucy wives even nipped occasionally at the cooking sherry while making supper.

Then there's sex. You may hear tales about the one-eyed, one-armed, one-legged Presbyterian parson in Texas who supposedly absconded with the wife of a deacon back in March of 1910 and refused to give her back. They say that the chase took them all over Mexico. It's not true.

And there was also the rumor that the synod of Northern New England was once forced into publicly denying that the Grace Metalious novel about the fictional town of Peyton Place was based on her observations of warm and loving Presbyterians. It also turned out not to be true.

For according to many outsiders, our loving denomination is a rather benign bunch. Well, yes, there was supposedly that genial elder in San Jose in 1960 who was brought up on charges of Quietness. He was said to have been sentenced to attend the session meetings even after his term expired.

And there was that pleasant Calvinist clergyman in a small town in upstate New York who was arrested in 1991 for jogging in the nude. People said it was his therapeutic way of sharing his feelings with his parishioners.

There have also been some recent unsubstantiated rumors about the use of a church photocopy machine for a personal purpose. They say an affable church administrative assistant copied her income tax form on it. But that's about it.

If you were looking for titillation, conniving, scandal, and general carryings-on, you should probably have joined our televangelist friends or got yourself reincarnated as a libertine. For we Presbyterians keep the Faith without undo money shenanigans, excessive stimulants, or improper sex. It's part of the Good Life!

PERCY T. PRESBY'S THOUGHTS ON REINCARNATION
Shirley MacLaine has never been—and will never be—a Presbyterian.

MARX MEETS CALVIN

You probably have heard that there are Presbyterians all over the world. There are churches in Latin America, Africa, Asia, and other continents. In fact, there are more Presbyterians in Korea than in the United States. And don't dismiss the story about the Presbyterians' flirtation with the Communists. It actually happened.

In 1941, the official stance of the Soviet Union embraced atheism. But the whole country, along with Premier Josef Stalin, was worried about the Nazi hordes that had invaded the nation that June and were advancing toward Moscow. There is some evidence that the West was not above exploiting the situation.

The dynamic Lord Beaverbrook was the British Minister of State and was visiting Moscow at the time. His colorful vocabulary was based on the Bible, and as the son of a Calvinist parson, he is reported to have pleaded with the dictator Stalin, "Promise me that if you become Christian, you'll become Presbyterian."

The conversation, of course, made its way back to 10 Downing Street in a diplomatic pouch, and eventually across the pond to the White House. But there, only those who were still turning on the landing lights for Amelia Earhart believed that it had any chance of actually happening.

You'll still hear some of the very old elders, though, speak in wistful awe about what it would have been like to organize the formal Reception of New Members Service at that time for more than 170 MILLION PEOPLE! It would have given new meaning to the phrase "God calls us all"!

SCHOOL DAYS

Presbyterians have always put a premium on higher education. Because of the "college" he founded in Geneva to extend his teachings, Calvin has been called a "Campus Minister." He endeavored to prepare "children for both the ministry and civil government" by insisting on a rigorous education.

This emphasis was carried on by his disciples. A member was encouraged to study, the better (in Calvin's words) to "judge the preaching against the authority in Scripture" and to raise the "standard of thought and discourse."

In the United States, the ministers and lay members embraced those notions with a vengeance. By the 1850s, the Presbyterians had founded 49 colleges in 21 of the then 34 states. They were equally influential in establishing many public institutions. Presbyterian Robert Bishop was instrumental in starting Miami (Ohio) University and John Monteith helped set up the University of Michigan. It got so that some believed that the Presbyterians were taking over public education.

In 1900, Woodrow Wilson was president of the prestigious

Presbyterian college—Princeton—before running for president of the United States. His successful campaign song was "School Days."

Today, there are some 67 institutions of higher education related to the governing body of the church. And according to surveys, 35 percent of our members are college graduates and 24 percent have graduate degrees. It all makes for sparkling and vigorous discourses and satisfies our inclination to talk every problem into submission in our beloved church.

PERCY T. PRESBY'S DEFINITION OF A PRESBYTERIAN #1

A Presbyterian is one who thinks that progress is okay as long as it doesn't change anything

5:00 Round Cookie Committee
Square Cookie Committee
Joint Cookie Committee

Chapter Two

MEETINGS AND COMMITTEES

PERCY T. PRESBY'S DEFINITION OF PRESBYTERIANISM

Presbyterianism is a series of meetings occasionally interrupted by a worship service.

MEETINGS, MEETINGS, MEETINGS

Our friends, the Catholics and Jews, think they attend an unusual number of meetings to deal with the vicissitudes of their religion. The Lutheran, Baptist, and certainly our Methodist cousins all gripe about all of the committee meetings they must attend.

But the hands-down winners in the meeting derby are the Presbyterians. According to Percy T. Presby, there are 22.2 meetings per capita held each year in the Presbyterian church. No other denomination even comes close.

And in spite of the many changes in our emerging new church, the small group gatherings haven't been altered that much over the years. The meetings are representative of our structure of church governance. To some observers, Presbyterianism is simply an ever-changing process with never ending procedures.

There are committees for almost every function in the denomination, and even one on the groups themselves. These are, of course, called the

Committees on Committees. Many of them are of the "standing" type, although why they all don't just sit down seems to continue to puzzle some people. They meet to decide the need for and the makeup of other committees, which study and make recommendations for solutions for which there are sometimes no problems.

Along the same lines, the General Assembly recently appointed a committee to study and review the General Assembly. It was evidently designed to act sorta' like comedian Tim Allen's "Tool Man" who developed tools for his tools.

But there are thousands of local committee meetings held every night at Presbyterian churches throughout the land. You probably won't want to change the number of meetings, for they are events where hearts are touched and spirits renewed. The gatherings have been going on for years. So when you join one of the existing groups, plunge right in. You'll grow to love it!

RUN FOR YOUR LIFE

People say that if two Presbyterians meet for the first time, they will form a brand new committee. It is therefore probably best to cross the street when you see another church member approaching.

PERCY T. PRESBY'S THEORY ABOUT THE CREATION

God so loved the world that He—or She—didn't wait for a committee to form it.

THE CAMEL COMMITTEE

There's an old saying that a camel is a horse that has been designed by a committee. You should probably remember, however, that the camel continues to amble majestically along—albeit a bit awkwardly. And the ship of the desert has staying power, patience, and grace.

HANDLING RESPONSIBILITY

Before you assume full-fledged duties on the many different committees in your new church, you may be asked to serve in various relatively minor positions. In a sense, you will sorta' be in training and your mettle will be somewhat tested to determine whether you can handle greater responsibility.

For example, you may be asked to be the helpful Keeper of the Sunshine Fund (for the choir) or the Plant Lady (for the annual church fair). In the former job, you will send flowers, cards, and plants to musical colleagues who are ill. In the latter position, you will admonish people to bring their plants indoors in the fall and ready them for sale at the event in the church basement. Although the duties may seem somewhat unimportant, they are emblematic of your commitment to—and fellowship with—your new comrades in the church.

But since one church group sometimes doesn't quite know what another is doing, the novice can end up being appointed to two or more positions. Some tasks are said to be a bit time consuming, so dual responsibilities are probably to be avoided whenever possible. After all, your entire church career is probably on the line here and you may be under some scrutiny. Remember that these duties are often but a prelude to being asked to join the hardworking and important Membership Committee to update the church membership list on your computer.

If you do get overloaded, you can occasionally escape an assignment by pleading a conflict of interest in the jobs. So unless you're really into both greeting cards and plants, you might try negotiating. But keep in mind that serving your fellow members—in at least one way—is the essence of God's good grace!

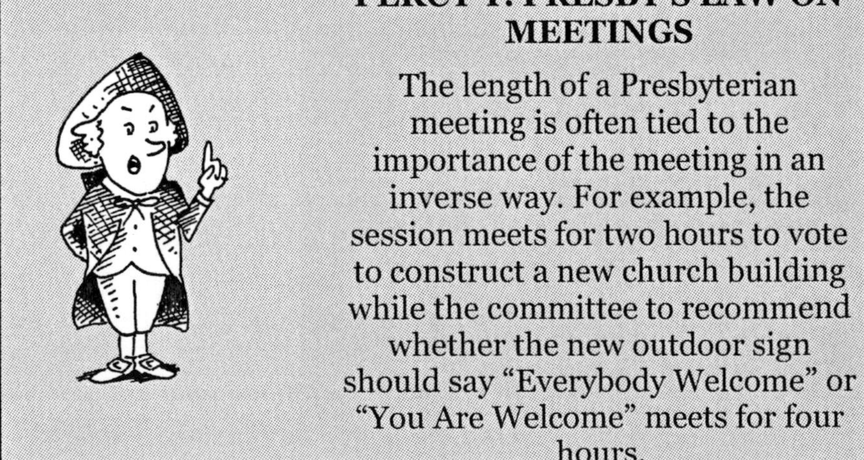

PERCY T. PRESBY'S LAW ON MEETINGS

The length of a Presbyterian meeting is often tied to the importance of the meeting in an inverse way. For example, the session meets for two hours to vote to construct a new church building while the committee to recommend whether the new outdoor sign should say "Everybody Welcome" or "You Are Welcome" meets for four hours.

SURVIVAL

Presbyterian committee meetings are sometimes long and dull. Not a few members reportedly stare at their papers with a glazed look in their eyes. Comedian Milton Berle once defined a committee as a group that keeps minutes and loses hours.

One way to survive is to contemplate rocket scientist Wernher von Braun's antidote for inaction. He was said to have recommended placing a stick of dynamite in the back of a stalled Volkswagen, where the engine was located. He answered his fellow passengers' indignant protests by shrugging that sure, it was bound to be messy, but it would darn well move the thing forward! You may have to suppress a smile at the thought of applying that technique to your chairperson's chair at a meeting. B - A - A - ROOM!

This rumination is recommended when your worthy leader is conducting a gathering with a thoroughness just this side of lunacy. Everyone will wonder why you're grinning so maniacally, and you might get into some interesting conversations in the parking lot after you all break up to prepare for the next meeting.

For there will be one. According to Presbyterian dogma, the Almighty wants it that way. And God still loves us. No kidding!

PERCY T. PRESBY'S THOUGHTS ABOUT MEETING DELIBERATIONS

If the Presbyterians had been in charge, Jesus would probably still be on trial.

AS I WAS SAYING…

If you become the chairperson of a Presbyterian committee, you are bound to look at things a bit differently. As the leader, you will probably have to come to grips with the notion that your group—while charming and dedicated—is also a bunch of well-meaning, but sometimes obstreperous individuals. They will most likely try your patience on some occasions.

For sure enough, just as you are moving things along during a meeting with your brand of benevolent dictatorship, one wonderfully earnest member will interrupt. It's bound to be the affable fella' who has committed every page of *Roberts Rules of Order* to memory. This helpful individual believes its contents are second only in importance to the Ten Commandments in keeping the Philistines from breaking down the doors. And he will interrupt you to make a "point of order."

If he's the only one conversant with the protocol of a meeting, you're relatively safe. Sometimes a little intimidating scowl will render him silent. But if there is another like him, you are probably in trouble.

The initial interruption will often escalate into an interminable wrangle over procedures, as each amiable member attempts to outpoint the other in quoting different rules. The argument may be somewhat long and a bit tedious.

It is useful at such times to remember the tale of the unflappable BBC announcer who was involved in the longest program interruption in history. It lasted seven years.

The British experimental television station went off the air on September 1, 1939, a casualty of the beginning of World War II. It was telecasting a Mickey Mouse cartoon at the time. The station returned to the air on June 7, 1946, with the same host that had introduced the cartoon seven years earlier. He turned to the camera with the remark, "As I was saying before I was so rudely interrupted…"

So let your wonderful committee members carry on their argument until they exhaust themselves in random acts of progress. Your time will come. You and the church will undoubtedly survive to hold another meeting on another day. And the blessings of it will be on all of us!

STAVING OFF THE INEVITABLE

Things move slowly in our denomination. We are a deliberate people. Leadership in our church is like steering around a corner in a big Mack truck, with a "slow-moving vehicle" sign on the back, rather than in a buzzing little sports car. An Episcopalian once remarked that if he learns that the end of the world is at hand, he will immediately become a Presbyterian because everything in that denomination takes a year longer!

PERCY T. PRESBY'S ADVICE TO COMMITTEE CHAIRPERSONS

If you are elected the chair of a committee, you should probably begin each meeting with that old Scottish prayer, "O Lord, grant that we may always be right, for thou knowest we will never change our minds."

HALLELUJAH, I WON!

If you become the chair of the Stewardship Committee, you will probably be called upon to devise some new ways to obtain money for your church. Innovative fund-raising ideas have a long history in our denomination, in spite of some official opposition to the practice. You may be tempted to try some games of chance. But our friends, the Catholics have cornered the market on bingo, the Jews on mah-jongg, and poker doesn't quite fit the image of good Presbyterianism.

In your search, you may hear about a smashingly successful experiment that was tried out West more than 70 years ago, although you would be well advised to steer clear of it. But just so you know:

The Presbyterian church in a little town in Nevada hit on a gimmick in the 1930s, and placed some unusual icons in the narthex of the church one Sunday. On that sunny morning, three gaudy slot machines welcomed the congregation to services.

Gambling, of course, was newly legal in Nevada, and in the dusty village of four casinos and bars, a gas station, and a general store, the good elders must have figured that if you can't beat 'em, join 'em!

Most folks thought that the machines were configured to further lower the odds against the players, because it was announced that all proceeds went to support the activities of the church. But on their way out on that (and subsequent) Sundays, many members and visiting sinners accepted the invitation printed on a big red sign above the slots that urged them to PULL A LEVER FOR JESUS!

They say that the result was an embarrassment of riches. The little church eventually got to contributing 80 percent of the suddenly swelling budget of the mission activities of the entire presbytery. It all went swimmingly until the General Assembly found out about the source of the newfound wealth, and put a stop to the idea that three cherries somehow represented the Trinity.

They evidently used the incident to remind all members of that ruling body's stand against any form of fund-raising for church activities. Instead, you are supposed to get people to give generously and repeatedly in proportion to their incomes. So you should probably curb any novel ideas about fund raising and borrow a begging bowl from your local public television station.

Or if you and your new local congregation feel really independent, please read on.

FUND-RAISING IDEAS

Some Presbyterian churches DO ignore the ban on fund-raising. If yours is one of them, you can perhaps bring some new ideas to the activity.

Now that the Bob Evans Restaurants have abandoned the International Chicken Flying Meet that used to be held in the little town of Rio Grande, Ohio, each spring, perhaps your congregation could sponsor a local version. All you need is some folk who have confidence in their fowl's ability to fly a bit, a ten-foot platform to serve as a launching pad for the birds, and a toilet plunger to give them a little gentle prod. The Humane Society can supervise things so that no chicken gets hurt. The one that flies the farthest wins. In addition to the entry fees, you can set up some bleachers and charge admission for the contest and for the chicken dinner afterwards.

If your church is on a hill and has a tall steeple, you might suggest that the congregation install a cellular phone transmitter on it, and lease it to a telecommunication company. The Old Whalers Church in Sag Harbor, New York, is doing just that. It gives new meaning to the phrase, "God's Calling You."

If you're particularly adventurous, you might suggest a variation of the Sheep-Shearing Day, which was held by the Fairmount, New Jersey, Presbyterian church for more than 20 years. They enticed as many as 5,000 city dwellers to drive out to a member's farm to watch the sheep being sheared. They called it "The One Great Hour of Shearing." Perhaps you could do the same with cows and call it "The Milk of Human Kindness Day." Yeee-haaa!

Or you could try mounting a "Jump for Jesus Jamboree!" You get some trampolines and...but you get the idea.

The point here is that you should not be timid in your recommendations, for there is no bottom to the well of bad ideas. And remember, when your idea bombs, there will probably be some obliging person there to remind you that they told you it would. God loves them also. Really! For we are one together in our faith-based community!

PERCY T. PRESBY'S THEORY ABOUT PLEDGING MONEY

Some Presbyterians watch he evening news in the hope that Tom Brokaw will tell them that Hell has frozen over; that way they won't have to make good on their pledge to the Stewardship Committee.

GIVING IT UP

Asking folks for money is a decidedly un-Presbyterian thing. So we sometimes use a sorta' indirect approach modeled after some old motel advertisements. We borrow from the Econolodge commercial that has it that "our costs are low, but our standards are high!" And as the old Motel 6 commercial proclaimed, even if you don't pledge—"we'll leave the light on for ya."

GRAB 'EM

Presbyterian Membership and Fellowship Committees have never openly advertised for new souls in the newspaper, of course, or lured people into the church promising soup and salvation. There's been no Huzzah! Huzzah! Huzzah! street corner proselytizing with a brass band or neighborhood doorbell ringing even in small towns. 'Twouldn't be seemly.

But if you become a member of such a committee, you will be told to look for the blessed new visitors in your church. There are a number of telltale signs. For example, they are usually better dressed and their hair is combed. They will begin the wrong tune to the Doxology and say *trespasses* instead of *debts* during the Lord's Prayer. They will smile nervously a lot, with a serious look on their faces. And they will put dollar bills in the collection plate instead of a pledge envelope. Hurry to their side immediately after the service and get those wonderful folk to the coffee hour!

THE SUNDAY STYLE

You may get on the Worship Committee at your local church. This important group determines the manner in which Sunday services are held. And it sometimes gets itself into delicious hassles with the pastor over where the authority of one begins and the other ends.

Unlike some other denominations, much of the order of things during worship and the style of devotions in the Presbyterian church is pretty much left up to the sessions and pastors of the individual congregations. There is no "definitive Reform theology of worship," according to church scholars.

Each local church, therefore, has its own character. Some traditional Presbyterian churches hold "high" services and some hold "low" depending on the extent of ritual. Our friends in Christ, the Catholics, will scoff at even the high type of service, however, for to them it resembles nothing more than a simple and stark New England town meeting.

Your membership on the committee will probably be both rewarding and vexing. Some of your warm-hearted colleagues may want to change some things around because they have become sleepy by the sameness of the service, which they feel has become occasionally boring over time. They seek creative contemporary worship services and new approaches in the proclamation of the Word. Others like things just the way they are—thank you very much.

So the differences in style are real. Writer Marva J. Dawn calls it all "the worship wars." Many churches revere the old traditional services. They seek to counter the 1990s youthful notion that you only have to do something once for it to qualify as "traditional."

But even they seem to want to tweak things a bit. Some of the recent heated discussions in those Worship Committees have occurred over whether to sing "Amen" at the end of every hymn or just after those whose words have been taken from the Psalms.

Other churches are experimenting with the so-called "blended worship" that combines modern praise music (using electric guitars, keyboards, and drums) with the old traditional hymns and other modern touches, resulting in a slightly altered service. There's even a guidebook about it all.

A few churches are expressing their faith imaginatively in affecting ways in a sort of avant-garde manner that is irrepressible and unpredictable. They seem to seek to imitate comedian Flip Wilson's old Church-of-What's-Happening-Now. "A Celebratory Dance on In-Line Skates" may give way to congregational participation in a "Bang-on-a-Can" service in which alarm clocks bing, egg beaters whirr, mason jars clink, cans thwunk, and other household appliances are brought to the service to make a joyful noise unto the Lord! The effect is like a small version of the noisy "Opus 21," the Hollywood welcome to the year 2000.

These gatherings are often designed by the Worship Committee to appeal to younger folks and baby boomers, with tambourines and happy-clappy music and clowns and short plays (called chancel dramas). It has made some older members look at one another in disbelief at the coffee hour, murmuring, "What WERE they thinking?"

Still other churches are returning to yesteryear and something deeper and less of the moment. In our age of speed, there is occasionally a move toward slowness. A few large churches are reportedly working toward a service that will embrace the magnificent Wagnerian spectacle of *Gesamtkunstwerk,* or *Total Art Work*, the supposed ultimate operatic fusion of music, drama, and image.

About the only apparent rule in the Order of Worship in most traditional Presbyterian churches, however, is that the offering should follow the sermon. It's evidently seen as a kind of litmus test for the preacher's work that morning.

So if you have a bit of a restless spirit you should probably begin to think about what you might suggest when you get on the Worship Committee. For it will then be partially up to you to contribute to the joy of bringing the Good News to all!

PERCY T. PRESBY'S DISCOVERY ABOUT CHURCH EFFICIENCY

They say that after a distinguished old member died, someone totted it up and discovered that he had served on 37 church committees at one time or another, and that 11 of them were said to have accomplished something!

BLESSED ARE THEY THAT FLEE

Sometime during your membership in the church, you may be asked to become the advisor to the youth group. As such, you will be asked to spend many of your waking hours with young people whose hormones are ricocheting through their bodies in no discernible pattern. Their kernels are still popping. So you will be working with a group of energetic young folks who are passing through a wonderful phase en route to the rest of their lives.

There is some indication that there is an invigorating youth rejuvenation occurring in our church. Attendance and participation in some local and regional gatherings have set records in the last few years. This is partly due to the passionate leadership and dynamic discipleship of our pastors and adult advisors. But there are some hazards.

As an adult advisor, you will probably have to accept the kids' fleeting assumption that their parents are really a bunch of dopes. The young of today seem to spend at least some of their waking hours hoping that they will temporarily become orphans.

At one time in the past, of course, it was different. Back in the days when both TV and morality were black and white, if you did something wrong, somebody would come along and beat up on your rear end. And kids listened. Today, about the only thing you can do is quietly suggest (to the boys-in-the-baggy-pants-with-their-underwear-showing) that they probably shouldn't wear rings in their body parts, and that it isn't cool for girls to keep reapplying and ladling on their new purple makeup.

Our Presbyterian kids, however, are usually a wonderfully gentle bunch. Some Baptist youth groups are known as the "Flock that Rocks" and the Catholics have their "Parish That Pulses." In the Presbyterian church, the youth group sometimes goes by the sobriquet the "Crew That Cuddles." A Rock-a-Thon fund-raiser by our mild-mannered Presbyterian youth often involves rocking chairs, not dancing.

You are bound to run into a few frisky kids, however, that will make you older in an hour. There's sometimes at least one mischievous lad who can't decide whether he wants to be the local salesman for the One and Only Original Kazoo Company of Eden, New York, or enroll in the Famous College for Locksmiths in Paducah, Kentucky. It all depends on the day. He also seems to be a member of the Church-of-Wearing-Your-Cap-Backwards.

You may have to deal with at least one delightful young lady who thinks gum is food and wears jeans so tight they give her a headache. Or perhaps, you may even have to counsel the minister's daughter, who has somehow developed a penchant for unsuitable crushes.

So unless you have infinite patience and seek rejuvenation yourself, it may be best to avoid the assignment, by being out of town or fleeing to the basement, when the committee comes calling to ask you to serve. Unless, of course, you have a wondrous teenager of your own.

Then you should probably consider becoming a youth advisor so you can listen and learn how great life is! For as Pastor John Underwood notes, "a church built on a rock may not be on a roll, but a church on a roll will most assuredly be built on a rock." And upon that rock (and roll) our youth will build their church!

PERCY T. PRESBY'S CERTAINTY ABOUT YOUTH DAY

When the vivacious adolescents take over the worship service on the annual Youth Day, it will be finished 20 minutes early, thereby throwing the elderly members of the Pioneers group, who are preparing the coffee hour for after-church that morning, into a complete tizzy.

CURB THOSE THOUGHTS

You may eventually be tapped to be ordained as a ruling elder in the church. This nomination (from a committee) for election to the post usually comes after a few years of faithful service. Both men and women are eligible, of course, but the individuals nominated must consider themselves worthy, for the responsibilities involve the actual management of local church affairs.

This usually results in some soul-searching on the part of the candidates before accepting the nomination. Percy T. Presby says that one kindly fellow in an Arizona church was so unnerved by the idea that he blurted out a confession. The committee was then forced to withdraw the invitation, reluctantly acknowledging that they shouldn't have anyone as an elder who had once had a few unspoken—but slightly improper—romantic thoughts about former Secretary of State Madeleine Albright. So you should probably best watch it!

BE PREPARED

After you've been around awhile as a deacon or elder, you may be elected to serve as the clerk (of session) or moderator (of the deacons). These are the top jobs and you will be in charge. Some folks say that you should then assume that you have probably heard the truth for the last time.

CALLED TO SERVE

There is no correlation between becoming a clerk or a moderator and being smart. A few such leaders often express regrets that they weren't smart enough to avoid becoming a clerk or moderator in the first place.

IN ORDER AND DECENCY

If you become a clerk or moderator, you may wish to lead your colleagues in the Presbyterian elder-and-deacon song, "In Order and Decency." It was written by Elder Bob Kottcamp in a fit of inspiration during a long committee meeting and is sung to the old French folk tune "*Vive le Compagnie.*" Try it out at your next meeting!

In Order and Decency

Verse 1

As elders and deacons we all lead our throng
In order and decency.
In meetings and meetings that are overlong
In order and decency.

Chorus

In order, in order, and decency
In order, in order, and decency
With polity and comity
And order and decency.

Verse 2

We deacons and elders will pass it along
In order and decency.
So sing all you people who want to belong
In order and decency.

Repeat Chorus

Verse 3

So come all you members, you cannot go wrong
In order and decency
Come on now and join in this wonderful song
In order and decency.

Repeat Chorus

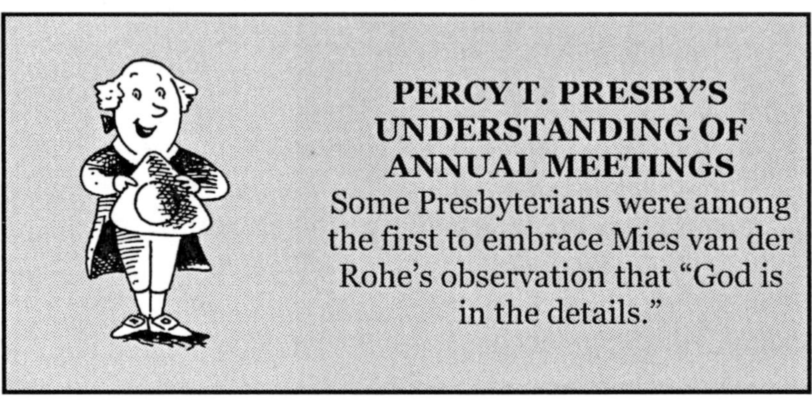

THE ANNUAL MEETING

How many Presbyterians does it take to change a light bulb? A quorum. So goes the old joke about the church.

This was—and is—especially true at the Annual Meeting of the local congregation. No business can be transacted unless a certain number of members are assembled. Some churches have been known to drag in passersby from the street with a promise of cookies and pink lemonade and other things of a more enticing nature, to try to make up the required numbers.

At the conclave, each diligent church committee makes a report, and the budget for the entire church for the following year is reviewed. The reports are often contained in a duplicated booklet that is compiled and made available to every member about a week before the meeting. The reports usually consist of one or two pages detailing what each group has accomplished during the past year—with God's help.

In spite of the fact that the reports could—and should—have been read by the congregation before—or even at—the meeting, some delightful committee chairpersons seem to be compelled to read the reports verbatim as if all of the membership is terribly illiterate. On occasion, however, an earnest few seek to jazz up the proceedings with exciting ad lib renditions of their group's work in the previous year.

Some say that because these verbal reports are supposed to last about five minutes and some of the amiable chairpersons have an attention span of a minute and a half, such efforts often leave a baffled membership to sort it all out. Not to mind. Confusion is good for the soul and few of your fellow members get in a dither—publicly anyway. Anyhow, oral reports often go on for at least ten minutes, which is why many Annual Meetings run at least two hours, regardless of the issues at stake.

And there will be a few. Some long-time participants say that if an issue is complex and no one understands it, there will probably be an immediate vote. If the issue is simple and easily understood, the debate over it will be longer than two Iowa politicians praising pork at a picnic.

At your first Annual Meeting, you should probably try to be quiet in order to get the lay of the land. Let others do the talking. As you become more Presbyterian, you will notice that you are fighting an almost irresistible urge to speak out. By the time your second Annual Meeting rolls around, you will be ready to take the floor with a blizzard of words! Your participation will then assure your full membership in what we lovingly call The-Church-of-the-Never-Ending Dialogue!

PERCY T. PRESBY'S THOUGHTS ABOUT ANNUAL MEETINGS

When it is apparent that the vote on an issue will be unanimous, there will usually be one negative vote, because many Presbyterians think that unanimity on anything is probably against God's will.

IHS

Chapter Three

PASTORS

PERCY T. PRESBY'S THOUGHTS ON THE MINISTRY

A Presbyterian minister is an agent of a higher power with a lower responsibility.

DON'T BLAME ME

Like that old song by Dorothy Fields and Jimmy McHugh, our pastors are said to have a wonderful out. When they encourage a member to pray to God for relief from troubles and things don't immediately work out right, they can remind them that God's delay is not God's denial. So "Don't Blame Me." Some folks say that anyhow, our ministers are in sales, not management.

TREAT THEM KINDLY

Although pastoral relations are an important part of the responsibility of every member of the church, they will be particularly significant if you become a member of the Personnel Committee. In that position, you must do your best to establish and maintain a good rapport with our ministers, lending those blessed people your continuing support.

For those dedicated folks have the unenviable task of shepherding a fascinating group of people through their spiritual life, staying one—but not two—steps in front of them. They must lead but not appear to do so, within an organizational structure that gives them very little power.

They say that Presbyterian parsons only have control of three things. They can choose the Scripture reading for a worship service and preach about it in the sermon. They can choose the hymns that accompany and reinforce the message. And they can decide whom to marry and bury.

Other than that, they have only one vote in the management of church affairs, and that's at the presbytery level, for they don't even belong to the church that they serve as minister. Oh, they can preside over the Annual Meeting of the congregation as the moderator for that assemblage, but that's about it.

Some churches boast that their church is a place "where every member is a minister." And some overzealous folks are said to take that too literally. This occasionally causes a few problems about who is, or who is not, in charge of what.

The pastor spends a lot of time in counseling, visiting the sick, in administration, and in serving *ex officio* on church committees. But the pastor's biggest influence on the fold is usually in the weekly sermon. In it, there is an opportunity to give us a glimpse of the divine as the preacher attempts to interface between our minds and our souls.

Every Saturday the clergyperson faces a blank piece of paper with a Scarlett O'Hara-like sigh that "tomorrow's another sermon." This is not your five-minute homily by our priestly friends in the Catholic church, but a full-fledged 20-or-more-minute oration that must inspire and challenge. The composition must be based on scripture and reach a high polemical fervor at least once.

The next morning, the pastor must put on a Sunday game face and once again do battle with the English language in public, while trying to render the complexities of theological thought in simple human terms. As Bruce Thielman notes, "To really, really preach is to die naked a little each time." And sure enough, just as the minister reaches the climactic height of the message, some baby will start to bawl.

Now, don't expect too much of your preacher. It's true that our church has had some spellbinders. One, George Whitfield (1714–1780), could reportedly bring tears to the eyes of his listeners by the way he pronounced *Mesopotamia*. And they say that evangelist Billy Sunday (1863–1935), who was an ordained Presbyterian minister, could make many of the ladies swoon with his soaring rhetoric. Some congregations have even dramatically responded to motions from the pulpit. At the Port Gibson, Mississippi, church, the favorite gesture of the preacher was a finger pointed to heaven. When he died in 1829, the congregation had a big finger carved in wood, embossed in gold, and mounted on the top of the steeple.

Today no Presbyterian church wants a tearful Jimmy Swaggart or someone who sounds like a 150-watt bulb screwed into a little reading lamp. But a little pizzazz wouldn't hurt, because no member wants to be like Eutychus in the Bible, who fell asleep and out of an upper window during a sermon.

But most congregations don't take to those preachers who hammer away at length in a blizzard of words. Although folks say that prolixity is something of an occupational hazard for all ministers, most members of Worship Committees in the Presbyterian church usually feel that brevity is one of God's greatest blessings. They are quick to suggest that succinctness is needed to prevent situations where the congregation stops listening to the sermon before the preacher stops preaching it.

And most Presbyterian ministers have learned in seminary that they shouldn't read their sermons, for as one wizened elder once remarked, "There were only three things wrong with this morning's message: (1) it was read; (2) it was read wrong; and (3) it was not worth reading."

The U.S. Navy has an old saying that ten percent never get the word. Some Presbyterian observers say that in church life, an equal percentage never get The Word. So as your spiritual leader, your minister must exhibit some pulpit power in helping you assess the present and see the unseeable, in our flight into the future.

Presbyterian pastors must also try to attend many of those committee meetings during the week. They must be ready to kindly and patiently explain parliamentary procedures to the genial (but occasionally bewildered) chairperson and mollify the warmhearted (but suddenly pugnacious) member who throws a conniption fit and demands that one of his colleagues be hanged for his remarks. Or at the very least be shipped off to the Presbyterian-Home-for-the-Terminally-Dumb, in Wahoo, Nebraska!

The clergyperson must also try to peaceably settle a little hassle over the date of the annual church fair and the mild brouhaha over who did or did not clean up the church kitchen last Thursday. When the session meets, the pastor can only hope that the newly elected elders will be newly enlightened. And when two of them get into a tiff over the amount of the sexton's cleaning fluid allowance, the minister must curb the urge to spank them both and send them to their rooms.

Then there are the administrative duties. The church office must be staffed, and they must occasionally settle the ever-so-polite arguments between the cheerful volunteers as to who is responsible for replacing the toner in the photocopy machine. If the clergyperson is in charge of a larger church, he or she must supervise a professional assistant or two or three other folks.

This sometimes means being called on to defend and counsel the eager young associate pastor who booked the local mortician as the guest speaker at the Pioneers' luncheon last week, and whose insights into his craft left most of the oldsters picking at their vegetables. This new seminary graduate is sometimes the same fellow who has trouble with his diction, ending many services with something that sounds like "Lettuce spray!"

But most of all, your minister will "minister" to the diverse needs of some wonderful and fascinating people within the local congregation. They say that the certifiable loonies are usually attracted to our friends, the Episcopalians, who, because of their English heritage, have a great tolerance for eccentrics. Many folk in the Sceptered Isle are said to wander lonely as a cloud, trying to keep from biting the moon.

But there are enough slightly goofy but delightful people wandering around in Presbyterian churches to keep the preachers compassionately concerned and alert. And to keep our clergy relishing the wide variety of marvelous folks in our beloved denomination. For we welcome everyone in Christ's name!

As Leader of the Pack, however, your minister must sometimes deal with the wistful widow who lives on Rhododendron Drive and sits in the back pew every Sunday with her friend. She whispers to everyone that the reason her slip is showing is that it's a signal for the Navy. At the coffee hour, her equally charming companion is prone to holler out—with no provocation—"Who had the veal cutlet?"

Then there's the enthusiastic but underdressed and overmedicated dilettante who has made the Presbyterian church her *cause d'jour,* along with the refreshing, newly arrived, oh-so-clever Korean family who have started up a Chinese restaurant near the high school called Wok and Roll. They want the minister to bless the grand opening. And the parson has to spend some time trying to straighten out the lovable fellow who thinks that Andy Rooney and Mickey Rooney are brothers and keeps getting them mixed up! (Andy was raised a Presbyterian.)

Some parsons reportedly have to try to help the terrifically giddy Sunday School teacher who thinks that the presidential heads on Mount Rushmore are a natural phenomenon and somehow believes that Elvis is alive and well and living with Big Foot in a Tibetan monastery. And they are sometimes required to deal with the jaunty lady usher who makes porcelain cream pitchers in the shape of a cow for a living and greets everyone with a cheery "Yippee Kai Yai Yo!" on Sabbath mornings, as well as the graceful Iowa farm wife of Italian heritage who has composed something she calls the "Dance of Lasagna." She'd like the choir to sing it some Sunday.

And then there's you. Be careful about imposing your ideas, problems, and sins on your local pastor. If you don't have any, don't make them up, the way they say some of our Catholic friends do in order to prove to the priest that they aren't some holier-than-thou-person.

Presbyterian ministers usually spend a great deal of time in formal and informal counseling. They sometimes have to try to help the gentle young fella' who understands all the rules to the Roller Derby and likes to attend Wrestlemania matches because his job as a library aide does not satisfy all of his emotional needs. And they sometimes have to counsel the terribly obese but fun-loving guy who, all by himself, disproves John Donne's assertion that no man is an island.

Because of their supposed liberal stand on many social issues, Presbyterian clergy must sometimes counsel delightful young ladies, some of who wear tube tops so tight that their contact lenses keep popping out. Many of them think that Chernobyl is Cher's full name, and they are sometimes on the rebound from some lad who played chopsticks with their affections and the process was so traumatic that it made their hair all frizzy.

Many Presbyterian pastors have to keep reminding themselves that some people say that God danced on the day that each of these folks were born. And that the Almighty continues to bless us all for our wondrous individuality!

Much of our pastors' counseling work, however, is with couples. They have long since learned how to deal with the Erich Segal generation who believed that love meant never having to say "I'm sorry." Now they spend a lot of time trying to teach couples, many of whom have three previous marriages between them, to say just that.

So the ministers must often have to remind themselves that their Christian duty is to embrace all of their lively and diverse members in a fellowship of love. For "by this, all men will know that you are my disciples, if you have love for one another." (John 13:35)

Certainly, Presbyterian ministers have days when they want to scream, but have to settle for a sigh. They are said to feel that they are the embodiment of that ancient Chinese curse, "May you live in interesting times!" As the revered Reverend W. Frank Harrington however, once noted, "I still hear trumpets in the morning."

But many of our pastors probably look forward to the day when they can retire from their strobe-like pace to the mountains of Montana where never is heard a discouraging word. Or to perhaps find some nighttime solace in the big and bright stars of Texas, as another song promises.

Most will find little comfort at that time in the words of W. C. Bennett of the Trinity Avenue Presbyterian Church of Durham, North Carolina. In what has become known as Bennett's Beatitude, he writes

Blessed is he who expects no gratitude,
for he shall not be disappointed!

So as a Personnel Committee member, treat the parson of your church with some kindness and sweet understanding while he or she is among you, before they go off to that last Great Potluck in the Sky.

This is particularly important if your minister is new to your church. They say that it takes an average of two years for a Nominating Committee to fill the pulpit of a Presbyterian church. Do not violate their innocence early.

Above all, don't be critical and demanding. Remember, our ministers are on our side!

THE PASTOR'S STUDY

The pastor's study is a symbol of the calling of the Christian minister to be the shepherd of a flock of God.

Here sermons are prepared to feed the congregation on God's Holy Word.

Here the work of the Church is planned so that the congregation may grow in grace and bear fruit in fellowship, teaching, and witnessing.

The pastor will not be surprised at your sins. Nor will he or she judge you by them.

But they will always invite you to share the wisdom and love of God, the knowledge of the forgiveness of sins, the saving grace of God in Christ Jesus, Our Lord. You are always welcome!

Anonymous

OUR PASTORS' CREED

Presbyterian ministers are said to believe that the first incidence of serial wrongdoing is an aberration, the second a coincidence, and the third, perhaps a pattern—maybe.

PERCY T. PRESBY'S UNDERSTANDING OF THE HAZARDS OF THE MINISTRY

For a Presbyterian parson, a counseling crisis is when the Kleenex dispenser stops working.

THE HOLY SHRUG

Many of our clergy are called to sometimes use the ecclesiastical "no comment" gesture. When a wrinkle of the forehead or a tilt of an eyebrow or a quiet downward look won't do, they sometimes resort to the holy shrug.

This little movement is used most often by our Presbyterian ministers when a slightly derogatory statement is made by one church member about another. The remark is often made to the pastor with the hope that it will elicit a sympathetic agreement about the person in question.

But since their mothers tried desperately not to raise foolish children, many of our pastors fall back on the little move of one shoulder. This expressive gesticulation does not imply a world-weary disdain or a total indifference or even a modern "whatever" to a member's biting remark. Rather, it is a time-tested gesture of patient ambiguity that can't be quoted or taken out of context.

The shrug, of course, has been perfected by the peoples of the Mediterranean. It is most often associated with the Italians, Jews, and of course, the French. And with the denizens of Brooklyn. But for many of our young pastors of an Anglo-Saxon background or those who don't come from that sacred New York place, the motion does not come naturally.

They don't teach the thing in seminary, so if you hail from that kind of wonderful ethnic heritage or location, give your new shepherd a break. If he or she hasn't picked up on it yet, teach them the subtle art of the little holy shrug. It will help God's ministry here on earth!

JUST SPELL IT RIGHT!

How would people respond to the idea of a Presbyterian pope? The fact is, we already have seven of them! That is, seven ministers in our denomination are named Pope.

Some years ago, Pastor John Underwood, inspired by an article in the now defunct *Presbyterian Survey,* studied the names of our clergy and in an inspired bit of whimsy, discovered that we may be able to glean some insights into our ministers and their ministry, by the study of their given names. With a sort of "it takes one to know one" attitude, he recently updated his research by perusing the 21,197 last names in the *Directory* (of Presbyterian Clergy) in Part III of the *Minutes of the 211th General Assembly (1999–2000).* Some are, of course, specialized clergy but many serve in local churches.

In addition to the seven Popes, he says, there are nine Bishops and five Abbots. Even two Priests are among our clergy. Three congregations evidently have a Layman in a ministerial role and three are served by Sextons. But surprisingly only five of our ministers are called Christian.

Still, one of our clergy is a Saint and another an Angel. Four are Rich and one is a Poorman. A whopping 119 are Brown, while 26 are Green, just outnumbering the 23 who are Gray. And there are two named Lavender and Peach.

One of our ministers is Old, but 52 are Young. Seven are Small and 16 are Little. But three are Smart, two are Wise, and one is Wiser. And one is Wild and another Wilder.

Two of our congregations apparently have a Ham in the pulpit and another has a Jester and one of our ministers is Bald. When it comes to preaching, 28 are Long but only four are Short, though two are Quick and one is Witty. Four are Frank, three are Bland, two are Lively, one is Fair—and another is called Ok.

But the eleven preachers named Love outnumber the seven who are Sweet and Strong. We have the religious seasons covered with one Easter, one Lent, and two Noel(s). And to make sure we all get to church on time there are 29 Bell(s). Three of our pastors are Meek but one is Meeker. And one embraces a wonderful name—Hug.

As the good Reverend Underwood points out, these names have been innocently imposed on their bearers—our given names are almost never chosen. And this wordplay, while amusing, is only incidental to the work of the clergy as they seek to make a name for all of us in Christ. Reverend Underwood urges us to Goforth (there are two pastors with that name) with Joy (one minister) all for the love of God!

FAMILIARITY

In the church in some parts of the United States, however, you may have to get used to calling the pastor by his or her FIRST name. Of course, you don't use Rabbi or Father, and you even drop the Mr. or Mrs. or Ms. And today, Reverend and Pastor are much too formal for some churches in our denomination.

No, in the egalitarian and progressive canons of some modern Presbyterian churches, it's Michael and Pamela. After a few months or so, you will probably be free to use the more intimate Mike and Pam.

Try it. Maybe you—and they—will like it!

PERCY T. PRESBY'S RECOMMENDED SILENT PRAYER BEFORE THE SERMON

Oh, Lord, let me speak the truth, but spare me from those who know it!

PRESBYTERIAN PREACHERS

Today's parsons are not cut from the same cloth as the two Presbyterian Johns. They're usually more benevolent, compassionate, and patient. It's helpful, however, to have some sense of where they are coming from.

The Swiss theologian Karl Barth once said that a good preacher stood with the Bible in one hand and the morning newspaper in the other. A story has it that one of our Baptist minister friends took that advice to heart, and preached 14 straight sermons on the Seventh Commandment with *The National Enquirer* in one hand and the Bible in the other. One of the married brethren finally went out and tried unsuccessfully to have a relationship with a woman who had three heads, just to see what in the heck the preacher was hollering about.

Probably for that reason, some Presbyterian preachers sometimes stand with the Good Book in one hand and *Roberts Rules of Order* in the other. No sense in tempting the Devil, they say.

YEP, IT'S ANOTHER MEETING

The burden of the unrelenting committee gatherings in the church parlors often falls heaviest on the ministers. Although they have no vote and usually exercise enormous restraint in their observation of democracy at work, they try to attend as many committee meetings as possible, in a valiant attempt to keep abreast of things.

So many parsons were falling asleep, however, that Percy T. Presby says that the San Francisco Theological Seminary began a series of courses in the mid-1970s to prepare soon-to-be ministers for the ordeal they were going to face. One was called "To the Brink." It consisted of a game in which the would-be clerics competed to see how close they could come to nodding off without actually doing so. Also introduced into the curriculum, he says, were courses titled "How to Shift Your Rear End Unnoticed" and "Things to Do with Your Hands." And they were also exposed to exercises to master the art of emitting a full-blown yawn without moving one's lips or squinching up the cheeks and eyes.

Many ministers did not take those courses, however, and often begin to drift off into the arms of Morpheus during committee gatherings. As a new member it is your duty to sit beside them at meetings and provide a discreet nudge or two when you see their eyes begin to glaze over. Keep the Spirit!

PERCY T. PRESBY'S LITTLE TRUISM ABOUT OUR PASTORS

During committee meetings, the ministers are probably the only ones who keep humming about all the trouble they've seen.

PASTORAL COMMITTEE PARTICIPATION

Presbyterian pastors are said to be adept at influencing decisions without appearing to do so. For some, it's an in-born skill. For others, there are supposedly some courses in seminaries that address the subject. Percy T. says that in those seminaries, pastoral arm-twisting is often called *consensus building*.

PERCY T. PRESBY'S IDEA OF PASTORAL HEAVEN

To preside over an annual meeting that begins with a motion to adjourn.

PASTORS' WIVES USUALLY GET PEEVISH WHEN

- ❑ people litter.
- ❑ bra straps show.
- ❑ their husbands are criticized.
- ❑ young men in tank tops eat with their caps on backwards in restaurants.
- ❑ they are awakened at one o'clock in the morning by a phone call from someone who wants to talk to their husband about the agenda for the next Peacemaking Committee meeting.

THE SPOUSES

Although some 23 percent of our Presbyterian ministers are women (and more females than men are now candidates for the clergy), the majority of the denomination's clergy are members of the male persuasion. Most of them have wives. And these persons are wonderful partners for their husbands. In fact, in the old days, when a church called a minister, they usually got two for one—a ready and engaging companion in all of his church endeavors. And at no extra charge. That pleased the session.

Today such expectations are foolish. It takes two incomes now to support a family, particularly if one of the incomes is a clergyman's salary. And many pastors' wives are dedicated to their own careers and jobs.

But it's helpful to understand where these admirable persons are coming from. They are not Cosmo girls and they don't look like the kind of woman who is trouble but may be worth it.

They don't wear purple. They do not know the word *flamboyant*. They don't dress like Madonna. They usually don't even wear dresses with barely-there spaghetti straps. They don't have personalized license plates. And their most extreme expletive is often "Gosh!"

They are, however, unpretentiously warmhearted and nurturingly compassionate. And they carry with them the fulfilling decency and kindness of God's sweet spirit.

The pastor's family sometimes includes the Presbyterian-issued blond, blue-eyed kids—a boy and a girl. When entertaining at home, the pastor's wife is adept at presenting a gourmet meal on a minister's salary and has the courage to serve broccoli, for it won't make that much of a dent in the bills folder she has on her desk, labeled "Due Unto Others."

In the old days, a pastor's wife's version of hell was setting the table without a desert fork. This is no longer true.

Today, she is usually a member of the church where her husband is the pastor, serves on committees, and often teaches Sunday School. For many years, a minister's wife was expected to play the piano, but that is also no longer a requirement.

What IS still required is an amazing amount of stamina, an enormous reserve of patience, and a ready coffee-hour smile. She must keep her composure in the most trying of situations and foster her own spiritual life amidst all the hullabaloo of a way-too-busy religious and daily schedule. And she must nod and smile at the enthusiastic flibbertigibbet who says that the last week's Annual Meeting was "electrifying."

(In fact, the said meeting was chaotic, giving credence to Dean Paul Lucey's observation that trying to chair a meeting of Presbyterians is like trying to take 80 kangaroos for a walk!)

So when you see the pastor's wife coming, break out your most welcoming smile. Give her a hug and a warm greeting. God—and she—will love you for it!

THE LILIES OF THE FIELD

Of course, pastors' wives have to watch their attire. But those women in our denomination who serve as ministers face an even bigger challenge—a challenge that has largely escaped our male clergy. How does a female member of the Presbyterian ministry present herself to the public? How does she strike a balance between decorum and style?

Simply put: What to wear?

Sunday mornings are not too much of a problem. A robe with perhaps the appropriate colorful stole is good. Many observers have noticed how much more naturally women pastors handle stairs in their pulpit robes. And many female clergy say that they wear low heels because they don't want to appear wobbly when they are moving around and in the pulpit. Most are said to pay some special attention to their hair, so the sunlight through the windows of the sanctuary won't accentuate the frizzies. And like their male counterparts, some female pastors in our denomination wear Roman collars on hospital visits to help the personnel there recognize that they are clergy.

In the civilian day-to-day world, a lot of our women ministers favor clerical black and white, sometimes in tailored pants suits. Or at least below-the-knee skirts. Black is a "today" color, and three-quarter sleeves are popular, so the clergywoman wearing something like that is inadvertently "in". And of course, power red is out.

Casual dress is another matter. Like their male counterparts, women pastors are role models and have to watch it. So they don't usually run from the gym to the post office in a tank top and exercise shorts. They must appear approachable but not provocative.

It's tempting to occasionally compliment one of our female Presbyterian ministers on her everyday attire. But often, one doesn't quite know what to say. And although they DO reap and sow, perhaps a mumbled something about the beauty of the lilies of the field might be in order.

TRY IT!

We Presbyterians are a rather shy lot. So some of us feel uncomfortable when our pastor asks us during (or after) the worship service to reach out and shake hands with those around us, greeting each other in peace in the name of Jesus Christ. You might even use that wonderful phrase in Senegal's native language, "Nang def." Its most accurate translation is not "How are you?" but "Do you have peace?"

So take a deep breath, smile, and say something—for the minister's sake. For in spite of what you may have heard, Presbyterian clergy are not immortal. And they say that each handshake that is prompted by a pastor is jotted down by an angel and goes a long way to ensure that minister's entry into heaven, where God will treat them better. Help our clergy out!

ENDURING THE UNENDURABLE

An old inside (and insightful) joke has recently been making the rounds among our Presbyterian clergy. A minister resigned and to comfort a distraught member, he said, "Don't be sad—your new pastor will no doubt be far better that I have been." But the parishioner continued to sob, blubbering, "That's what the one before you said!"

PERCY T. PRESBY'S RECOMMENDED EPITAPH FOR OUR PRESBYTERIAN PASTORS

He—or she—has gone to another meeting.

Chapter Four

WORSHIP

PERCY T. PRESBY'S WARNING ON PROMPTNESS

Since John Calvin's day, no Annual Meeting, committee gathering, or worship service has ever started on time; all who dare to break this tradition will find that their toes have rotted off.

CALM DOWN NOW

Remember that restraint in all things is very Presbyterian. This is particularly true during our worship services. Sometimes, however, things can seem to get a bit dull. So after you've been a member for a while, you'll probably begin to harbor a dirty little desire for some pageantry in your religious life.

Not the minor-key purple beauty of a cantor's chant during the parade of the Torah. Not the magnificent procession of brilliantly colored vestments and the bells and smells and choreography of the Roman Catholic High Mass. Certainly not the veneration of icons and kneeling and beards and headdresses and incense of the Eastern Orthodox Church. Those wonderful services often smack of pagan rituals to an envious Presbyterian's eyes.

Some of our churches ARE experimenting with innovative new ways of worship. They seek different approaches in bringing the Good News to the congregants. But our traditional churches usually don't go for some of the new-fangled, atonal Christian music with repetitive rhythmic patterns that are danced to by the choir during the procession down the aisle. And they can't relate to the wondrous choreography accompanying the singing of the anthem in Micronesian do-wop. Or to the Sunday School kids' parade around the sanctuary celebrating the spiritual significance of Silly Putty.

But as a change from the vanilla-ice-cream Calvinist services, you'll find that even some of the older members secretly wish for at least some strawberry topping. The closest we usually get is the choir processing with candles on Christmas Eve.

A stark white simplicity somehow seems more proper in the traditional Presbyterian way of things. But even the older member's heart has been known to beat a little faster when the pastor wears a pulpit robe and a little child lights two candles to begin services. God loves us—and we're learning to try some new things. Rejoice!

TRY IT—YOU'LL LIKE IT!

Even if you hew to the old-fashioned services, you might want to help your church introduce some modern, cheerful variations of traditional music to the Sunday morning gathering. Two Presbyterian songsters, Charlene Cosman and Barbara Hussey, suggest singing the Doxology to the tune of "Chim Chim Cheree." Try it!

Praise God from whom all blessings flow
Praise Him all creatures here below.
Praise Him above, ye Heavenly Hosts
Praise Father, Son, and Holy Ghost. Amen.

Or you might try it to the tune of "Hernando's Hideaway" from *Damn Yankees*. It's one way to get other lighthearted folks involved!

PERCY T. PRESBY'S LAMENT ABOUT INVOLVEMENT

Many Presbyterians seem to want to sit in the front of the theater but in the back of the church.

ON CHURCH ATTENDANCE

Our brothers and sisters in Christ, the Catholics and Episcopalians, have to attend and receive the Holy Eucharist every week or someone will sneak into their homes some night and rearrange the little magnets holding the schedules on their refrigerator doors. Although 64 percent of Presbyterians say they attend church "weekly or almost weekly," we obviously do skip services once in a while. Doing so means that we can occasionally revel in the feeling that we are getting away with something.

This can be the basis for some drowsy Sunday mornings in bed with the scattered papers and a second cup of coffee. You can cuddle up to the fact that you don't have to be anywhere until Monday morning!

But be prepared to feel guilty when the rest of the family comes home and the kids show you what they made in Sunday School.

AMAZING GUILT

God does love us sinners. When you feel particularly bad about not attending church services on a Sunday morning, you might atone by warbling "Amazing Grace" to yourself in the shower, to the tune of the opening theme of *Gilligan's Island.* Try it in a really slow tempo, but with a little beat.

Amazing grace, how sweet the sound
That saved a wretch like me
I once was lost, but now am found
Was blind, but now I see.

Or you might try it with a sorta' southern accent to the theme from *The Mickey Mouse Club.*

A-M-A-Z-I-N -G-R-A-C-E
Amazin' Grace (How sweet the sound)
Amazin' Grace (How sweet the sound)
That saved a wretch like me
I once was lost but now am found
Was blind but now I see
A-M-A-Z-I-N-G-R-A-C-E!

Either way, singing that beautiful old hymn to a new tune might make you want to scurry back to the traditional melody at church next Sunday!

SACRED TIME

Sometimes, of course, you are forced to make a choice about Sunday morning services. As a soccer parent or a Little League baseball coach, it's often either the church or the playing field.

Time was when the so-called " blue laws" forced all stores to close on Sundays and denominational traditions in many faiths kept activities at a minimum. Nowadays, a lot of the sports and other activities that teach many wonderful things to our young are held on Sunday mornings.

So it's a real dilemma. How can you and your kids be faithful and still play? The Reverend Tom Goodhue of the Long Island Council of Churches recommends that you and other interested folks meet with the clergy on an interfaith basis to reach a consensus in scheduling weekend sports to accommodate worship and religious education. Then it's hopefully, "PLAY BALL!"

BLESSED ARE THE LITTLE ONES

When you do attend church services regularly you may end up being involved with Sunday School. You may not be able to duck this responsibility, for at one time or another you will probably be asked to be a teacher.

Not to worry. The church will provide you with all sorts of curriculum materials. In fact, you will be so inundated with them that you will probably have a hard time sorting them all out.

But your local Christian Education Committee has some goals and objectives that have been carefully planned. All you have to do is handle the frisky kids. And since some may have had to be persuaded to come to the building with the big plus sign on it, you may have a problem.

There is often a cute Dennis the Menace type who can drive you bananas. He thinks God's last name is "Forbid." And characters like those in the long-running Peanuts comic strip (which was drawn by the late Charles Schulz, who was a Presbyterian) are often there. But this is not the funny papers!

In reality, there will be some vivacious kids who are a handful and whose sole purpose seems to be to make your Sunday mornings seem like you're being churned by one of those paint-mixing machines! They won't listen to your carefully prepared lesson, they won't work quietly alone, and they won't cooperate with the other kids!

But now and then, you'll get a wonderful glimmer of God's presence here on earth. Percy T. Presby spent some time in a church classroom trying to teach the Lord's Prayer. And over the years, he has collected some of the little kids' versions and combined them with versions heard by other teachers. The result is what he calls "A Little Girl's Lord's Prayer."

A LITTLE GIRL'S LORD'S PRAYER

Our Father, whose Art in heaven,
Harold would be thy name.
Thy kings do come,
Thy Will B. Dunn,
On earth, as it is in Hopewell.
Give us this day our daily breadth
And forgive us our sons
As we forget one another.
And lead us not into Penn Station
But deliver us from e-mail.
For thine is the King Dome
And the powders of Gloria, forever.
Ah, Men!

LOOKING FOR A DRY EYE IN THE HOUSE

When you do attend church, you'll find that Presbyterianism offers the possibilities of a collective uncorking of emotions and some major sobbing opportunities. They are seldom exploited, though. A moist eye and some sniffles are just about as far as we Presbys are wont to go.

If you are of a sentimental nature, however, you have to be careful. A few worship services can be divided into one, two, or three-handkerchief occasions. You should probably be aware of the possible threat to your laundry.

In the one-hanky category is the Carol Choir rendition of "Jesus Loves Me" on Children's Day. The starched dresses and shiny Mary Janes of the girls and the scrubbed look of the boys make a lot of members sniff at their reencounter with childhood innocence. The song itself has been known to destroy a few grandparents, even when the group wears choir robes, and baggy jeans and dirty tennis shoes peak out from underneath the robes.

A two-handkerchief rating goes to the baptismal service after which the pastor carries a newly anointed baby in a 100-year-old lace gown up and down the aisle for the elderly to gently touch while everybody sings "Jesus, friend, so kind and gentle, little ones we bring to thee." It's a grabber!

Hardly anyone can stay clear-eyed on Christmas Eve when a second-grader in his bathrobe escorts a Mary (carrying "Stupid Julie Oppenlander's dumb ol' doll") to the creche, while little treble voices sing "Away in a Manger." It's a genuine three- handkerchief, transcendent, warm and fuzzy moment of peace!

Plan on sniffing and looking at the ceiling a lot during these services. Everyone will think you are seeking divine inspiration!

SINS

By now, you probably know that becoming a Presbyterian doesn't necessarily mean that you will not be an occasional sinner. But it does guarantee that whatever you may do, you will not enjoy it.

CONFESSION

Sins in the Presbyterian church are usually not hard to get. But they are also not hard to lose. All you do is join in the reading of the general confession in the bulletin every Sunday with everybody else. Then the worship assistant or the pastor says that we're all forgiven, we sing "Glory Be to the Father," and everybody sits down.

There is no individual confession as in the Catholic church, where one is accountable for specific violations—real or imagined —of God's laws. And we don't have to say a lot of prayers or light candles all next week as penance.

No, in our church you just join in mumbling the written general confession on Sunday that covers just about everything imaginable without getting down to the real nitty gritty personal stuff. That's for you and your conscience.

When you leave church every Sunday, however, you are supposedly free of sin and you will definitely not go to hell—at least for the time being. You'll have even been forgiven for that little fib you told someone yesterday.

But you usually have to watch it all week long. During some weeks, next Sunday seems to be a year away!

PERCY T. PRESBY'S THOUGHTS ON ATONEMENT

Catholics cannot fathom the Presbyterian group confession that ends with everybody absolving themselves.

A LOAF OF BREAD, A JUG OF WINE

About this Communion thing. Of course you know it celebrates the Last Supper and the body (bread) and blood (wine) of Jesus. Along with Baptism, it's one of the basic sacraments in all Christian churches. The idea is to eat some bread and drink some wine to remember that Christ died for our sins.

Every faith has its own special version of the event. Some of the new nondenominational megachurches are rumored to serve the wine with little umbrellas. Even within a denomination, the ritual may vary from local church to local church, but some generalizations can be made.

Catholics usually use little wafers for the bread, as do the Episcopalians and some Lutheran churches. As you move farther away from Catholicism, you begin to run into bite-size pieces of Wonder Bread, and by the time you get to the Presbyterians, it's sometimes fresh-baked loaves of whole wheat with cinnamon, raisins, and pecans.

Our brothers and sisters in Christ, the Lutherans, serve real wine in glasses so tiny you can't get your fingers around them. And although it isn't a very good vintage, the combination of a piece of bread and a shot of wine has been known to make more than a few empty stomachs rumble, early on a Sunday morn. We Presbyterians use the little glasses, too.

Our colleagues, the Catholics and Episcopalians however, seem to be afraid of people spilling them and ruining the carpet, so everybody marches up and gets a sip from a goblet held by the priest, or sometimes he just dunks a wafer in the wine and puts it in your mouth. It's still real wine, though, and most connoisseurs give an edge to the nectar served by the Episcopalians, who are renowned oenophiles.

As a Presbyterian, though, you're probably going to get pure unadulterated Welch's grape juice. Although Jesus turned water into wine as his first miracle (John 2:1), modern-day Presbyterians usually shun the nectar from the ground. Wine was used in Presbyterian colonial America, for there was no such thing as grape juice. But the Temperance Movement of the late 1800s and early 1900s persuaded many of today's sessions to believe that a shot of the real stuff might possibly lead to some unseemly thoughts.

But you usually won't have to go get the grape juice. In most Presbyterian churches, you still just sit there in the pew and the elders and deacons pass among the congregation with the little glasses and the bread. You are supposed to select a cube or break off a hunk as it is passed and pick up one of the tiny glasses.

Sometimes, though, we serve communion like our friends, the Catholics, Episcopalians, and Lutherans, who often make you get up and shuffle to the altar in order to get the sacraments. In essence, the communicants go to God, rather than God having come to them.

The farther you get away from those denominations, however, the more they come to you to serve communion. They say that in some modern Fundamentalist churches, they'll bring it right out to your car or pickup.

The only tricky thing about this whole deal in the Presbyterian church is knowing exactly when to actually eat the bread and quaff the juice. Listen closely, because the ancient passages explaining the significance of the various steps are sometimes mumbled by the minister, who's been through it lots of times. But watch his or her hands. They know what they're doing.

One last thing. On the back of the pew directly in front of you there will often be a little shelf with holes in it. You place the empty glass in one of the holes after you do the bottoms-up bit.

Two hundred people doing this more or less simultaneously sets off a soft clunking effect that is somewhat unsettling to the nerves on a quiet Sabbath morn. If you're a former Catholic or Episcopalian, though, the sound will remind you of the bangs that resound when the prayer kneelers are pushed back up. Feel at home!

BAPTISMS

Another one of the sacraments in the Presbyterian church is Baptism. We usually don't wait until people are grown up and dunk 'em in the river like our comrades in the Baptist church. We figure kids are simply short adults, so we just sprinkle a few drops on the baby's head and call it done. Waste not, want not, you know.

PERCY T. PRESBY'S LESSON FROM BAPTISMS

Presbyterian girl babies are often named Heather or Muffin because their mothers think the appellation sounds just darling and their fathers strategize that no man will ever be able to fire a girl with such a cute name!

SNOW IN THE DESERT

As a Presbyterian, you're probably going to run into some perplexing inconsistencies and misunderstood music lyrics. They will often crop up at worship services during Christmas time.

Like when a precious little one substitutes "Barney's the King of Israel" for the last line of "The First Noel." Or another peanut sings that Santa's "making a list of chicken and rice."

And here you are celebrating the birth of a baby that took place in a hot, dry, arid land full of sand and scrub. How does that reality square with the choir's anthem that begins with the line, "The snow lay on the ground…" to describe the scene in Bethlehem? And how do you reconcile the image of a bunch of people walking around in the robes and sandals of that day with the wintry Victorian Christmas cards you just sent out?

Don't try to explain it all to your kid. Leave that to the poor Sunday School teachers. And hey, nobody said this Presbyterian thing was going to be easy!

SING OUT!

Presbyterians do sing! While we don't much go for the bump-de-bump gospel music of our Baptist friends or the Irish-American repertoire of our Catholic colleagues, we have been known to amiably stumble over and around a melody during a worship service.

To help things along there's a hymnal. And as you may have heard, there's "the new one." Its cover is Presbyterian blue, replacing the maroon-look of the old hymnal. The new one is, in fact, the third one in more than a half-century, and it has all sorts of changes in it. Enough of them so as to have made it just a bit controversial when it was introduced in 1990.

Its creation took a bit of doing. A national committee of 18 stalwart souls worked on the thing for four whole years, holding 17 meetings around the country. There were also countless subcommittees hard at work all during that time.

The group was not above taking advantage of the labor of others. After all, there are more than 800,000 hymns from which to choose.* The committee seemed to have waited for our comrades, the Baptists, Episcopalians, and Methodists, to make their choices and finish their new hymnals before launching the new Presbyterian version.

It's been noted that Vivaldi didn't write 500 pieces of music, but only one piece 500 times. The hymnal committee evidently bought that idea and, citing the sameness of much of the previous editions, opted for a more diverse collection of songs. They said they were being more "inclusive." They chose 600 hymns, of which 180 are new.

When they first tried it out, some church members thought that the new book simply proved that the walls of Jericho were once again tumbling down. Others praised its different approach. The reaction to it was often an indication of the age of the member.

No, there isn't any twangy, catch-in-the-throat sob of honky-tonk country, or black rap syntax, or even the Puccini-like melodies of Andrew Lloyd Webber in it. But there are some new tunes that will make you not want to believe your ears. One of them sounds like a hard-rock number played backward, written by someone who was having a nervous breakdown!

In an endeavor to be less militaristic and sexist, the committee dropped some of the old traditional favorites. The Christmas carol, "God Rest Ye Merry Gentleman," went, as did "Faith of Our Fathers." And "Onward Christian Soldiers" and the historic "Battle Hymn of the

---

*Some 600 of them were written in the mid-1800s by a Presbyterian with the wonderful name of Horatius Bonar. Another Calvinist, John Hastings of the Bleeker Street Church in New York City, composed 1,000 during the same period.

Republic" were jettisoned. Some others were dropped—those that had been repeated so often at services that they had begun to sound nostalgic.

In their places are some NEW melodies that sound somewhat old-fashioned. In all, it's an earnest Christian attempt to be more "with it."

But not to worry. If you're new to the church, you will find the hymnal exhilarating, refreshing, and quite inspiring. It will lift your spirits!

So stand up and sing out the songs in the new hymnal, even if you're a bit off-key. It's best in these matters to follow the directives of John Wesley, the founder of Methodism. He advised his followers not to be ashamed of being heard and to "sing lustily and with good courage." If we do so, perhaps God will think we're all Methodists and let us into heaven sooner!

PERCY T. PRESBY'S DEFINITION OF A PRESBYTERIAN #2

A Presbyterian is one who thinks that singing "Rock of Ages"* is just about as close to today's pop music as one should get!

ON READING SCRIPTURE

After you've been a part of the church awhile, you may be asked to read from the Scriptures on a Sunday morning. You are expected to read the passages in the original Presbyterian. You should approach this assignment with caution. Stick to the text as written, however arcane

*written by member Augustus Toplady in the mid-1700s.

the language and obscure the meaning. If you're assigned that peculiar passage from Job that goes

> *I am a brother to dragons, and a companion to owls.*
> *My skin is black upon me, and my bones are burned*
> *with heat. My harp also is turned to mourning, and*
> *my organ into the voice of them that weep.*

Don't think about it! Don't shake your head! Just read it! And do not try to make your rendering of the beautiful poetry understandable by introducing the passages in colloquial English. Don't present the tale of the Wise Men and their travels as the story of "three fellows who walked nearly all night to get to a barn." When your assignment is the story of the Good Samaritan, don't characterize him as "the first do-gooder to come down the pike." And don't introduce Judges 16 by noting that Delilah was probably the world's first militantly feminist barber!

Above all, don't add editorial comments to your delivery. Reading the tale of Lot's wife before the congregation at 11:20 A.M. on a sunny Sabbath is not the time to wonder aloud why she was turned to salt and not pepper. And you should not interpret the biblical statement that on the seventh day "God rested" to infer that the Almighty went off someplace to take a nap!

No, just get up there and recite the words in a firm and measured tone, like those who have read the beautiful passages before you, in centuries past. And you should try to look like you understand what you're reading.

We Presbyterians want it that way. Like our lives, we prefer our scripture straight, unvarnished and just a bit cloudy, so that the preacher can explain it all to us in the sermon.

For as the Reverend Peter J. Gomes, Minister to Harvard University, reminds us, "The dynamic quality of the scripture has to do with the fact that while the text itself does not change, we who read the text DO change—the text adapts itself to our capacity to hear it."

PERCY T. PRESBY'S ADVICE ON SILENT PRAYER

Presbyterians should probably take Oral Roberts's advice that when you are talking to God, be sure and ask for something big, so as not to waste the long-distance charges.

PRAY FOR ME

Although you shouldn't pray out loud by yourself in a Presbyterian church, you sometimes do have an outlet. Your pastor is your mouthpiece. He or she can perhaps get through the din of daily life and reach the Almighty.

Some Worship Committees in some churches have set aside a period right after the Sunday sermon for Prayers of Intercession, Concern, and Celebration commonly known as Joys and Concerns. It can be—and often is—the minister's finest hour.

In some churches the clergypersons climb down from the pulpit and roam the aisles, soliciting news, celebrations, thoughts, and concerns as well as the names of people to pray for that morning. Some churches provide prayer request cards to give to an usher or the pastor.

But ministers also usually pre-arm themselves with a so-called short list. This contains the names of members or their relatives who are in the hospital or have died during the last week. It's used in the event that the current Sunday's flock is unaccountably tongue-tied—to sort of prime the pump.

In the congregations that follow this practice, it usually does take some time to get the ball rolling. But the longer the floor is open for suggestions, the more they are proffered. People seem to overcome their initial reluctance when they hear some of the ideas offered up by those around them.

For the suggestions often range from the poignant to the self-serving to the trivial. A concern for our servicemen abroad may be followed by a request that a prayer be said so that it doesn't rain on the town's yard sale that afternoon. A gracious matron tentatively asks that a little prayer of thanksgiving be offered up in celebration of her silver wedding anniversary (although privately she's not sure if the event is a joy or concern) while an old codger wants the Lord to intercede with those scoundrels in Washington who are ruining the economy!

Another somewhat puffed up member wants some thanks given because he and his family have just returned safely from their vacation in which they visited nine states and five cities and saw the tomb of the twelfth President of the United States as well as Alligator Park and Walt Disney World!

The genial local salesman for smoke alarms requests that some sort of mention should be made to God about the essential need for people to be more prepared for disasters—such as fires. Someone else wants a prayer said for the door-to-door missionaries the General Assembly is sending to Salt Lake City, and one of the kids thinks the Lord ought to know that the balloon animal she got at the party last Friday is slowly dying of asphyxiation.

Mixed up in all of this are suggestions for other prayers of celebration for birthdays and graduations, and there's inevitably one for the choir. There's usually a hidden reason behind THAT one!

During all this activity, the minister has been frantically making notes on the back of a bulletin, and now—IT'S SHOWTIME!

The pastor's got to juggle all of the suggestions around and weave them into some coherent whole. On the spot! With no rehearsal! In front of God and everybody!

In some communities, people have been known to attend the Presbyterian church for just this instant. It's the Calvinist version of the Moment of Truth! Instead of a bull, the minister faces the dangers of a loss of memory, lack of vocabulary, and incomprehensible inappropriateness! Alone! And unarmed!

Eyes half-closed and squinting at the notes, the preacher's got to tread spontaneously through the minefield of the congregation's needs and joys and concerns. Remembering all suggestions, he or she must comfort the bereaved, give solace to the ailing, celebrate the joys of life, and somehow make the inconsequential consequential. All in about five minutes!

Everyone agrees it brings a sense of excitement to the service. The suspense is exhilarating! Will the parson forget one? How will the preacher get out of that political suggestion? What has the Lord got to do with balloons?

Some congregations have reportedly taken to informally rating their pastor's performance during this time. They measure the merging of diverse needs, the ease of the transitions, and the spiritual rhetoric. The gestures, voice quality, patterns of improvisation, and attempts to make the insignificant significant bring smiles or frowns to the bowed heads as their spiritual leader weaves a torturous way to a prayerful conclusion.

A few churches are said to have gone so far as to issue placards (numbered from 1 to 10) at the beginning of services. During the last verse of the final hymn, the congregation raises aloft their individual scores for the Pastoral Prayer of the Day. One of the deacons jots them down and later averages them out.

According to Percy T. Presby, the highest score to date was a 9.0. The feat was accomplished by a pastor in Oklahoma who managed to include 15 of her parishioners' suggestions in an eight-minute tour de force that reached a climax with a rousing prayer for the success of the building fund. He says that the congregation leaped to its collective feet and gave her a very un-Presbyterian-like Standing O!

So do not despair. Your individual prayers need not be said in silence. If your local church doesn't follow this custom, perhaps you could mention the possibility to someone on the session. Only be sure to get the minister's approval first. A few of the younger ones have been reported to faint dead away at the mere thought of the idea.

SING, YOU SINNER

If you've ever sung in a high school choir and mention it in passing to any member of your new church, you're probably in trouble. Even if your sole contribution to music today is an occasional burst of bravado in the shower, you can expect to be gently besieged to join the choir. They're always looking for new members to sing at worship services, quoting St. Augustine to the effect that "he who sings, prays twice."

You will be as heavily recruited as a star athlete by a college, for to some Presbyterian churches, their music program is as important as a sports program is to a university. Instead of an Athletic Director there is a Minister of Music and some larger churches have three choirs. They are sometimes called the Carol or Cherub (for wee ones), the Westminster or Junior (for adolescents), and the Chancel or Senior (for older warblers). In the South, where religion is taken so seriously that the newspapers sometimes rate churches like they rate restaurants, a good music program goes a long way toward four stars!

You will be in particular demand if you happen to be a tenor. Sopranos sing the melody and a lot of people can hack that, and as they get older, women's voices frequently become lower so they sometimes become altos. And to sing bass is just to engage in sustained talking at a deeply masculine level, to paraphrase Professor Harold Hill.

Singing tenor is quite another matter. In addition to a high voice, you need to read music above the staff. Church choirs are in such dire need of tenors that they will sometimes tell a prospect that as a signing-up bonus, he doesn't need to bring a covered dish to the next potluck dinner.

Be aware, however, that there are no scholarships, and only a few lead members in some big-city churches are paid. And you'll have to give up Thursday evenings for rehearsals. No Presbyterian choir member ever saw the first-run episodes of *Seinfeld.*

And just being a choir member doesn't make you extra pious. When people say that the parson is "preaching to the choir," it's often more of a tribute to their consistent attendance than to their religiosity.

But to sing is God's greatest gift! If you're a bit shy about sharing your modest talents, remember Thoreau's observation, that "the woods would be very silent if no birds sang there except those that sing the best!"

PERCY T. PRESBY'S LAW OF PROBABILITY ABOUT MUSIC LEADERS

The Presbyterian choir director who chooses more than five anthems in Latin in one year will probably not be the choir director the next year, but a spirited arrangement of "Ta-Ra-Ra-BOOM-Dee-AY" will probably not be welcomed by even the most progressive Presbyterian congregation.

ON APPROBATION

There may be some times during some worship services in your new church when you might feel like clapping. The urge may come upon you spontaneously after a particular stirring and happy announcement of joyous news, ending in an upbeat phrase that almost demands some enthusiastic response! It's also hard to sit on your hands when the frisky high school kids do a skit promoting their fund-raising activity that ends in a Hollywood-shtick kind of finish. And it is difficult to refrain from showing your appreciation to the choir in a large church, after their fine rendition at Christmas time of Handel's "Hallelujah Chorus."

But you probably should try to restrain yourself. You are in God's temple. And according to old Presbyterian dogma, the Almighty doesn't need applause. Although this is changing somewhat in today's church, you should probably continue to keep the spirit with the joy of the sound of one hand clapping.

Chapter Five

THE MEN AND WOMEN

PERCY T. PRESBY'S DISCOVERY ABOUT FEMALES PAST

Folks used to say that in the traditional world of Presbyterian women, "horses sweat, men perspire, and women glow" so indeed God "made everything suitable for its time." (Ecclesiastes 3:11)

PARADISE FOUND

According to the Good Book, Man lay down in a deep sleep in the Garden of Eden. One of his ribs was extracted, and Woman was created. Mark Twain said Adam then complained that the new creature with the long hair immediately displayed a penchant for naming everything in the world—including all imaginable colors.

Some say that when God invented Man, She was only testing things out. So when things didn't quite work out right, Presbyterian women have traditionally justified any erratic behavior on their part by the fact that they were created from the most crooked part of man.

And then, as many point out, the tribes wandered for 40 days and 40 nights in the wilderness because some dumb guy refused to stop and ask for directions. It served to remind everybody that women are interested in the simple things in life—like men. Many feel that there has been only one indispensable one—Adam.

Presbyterian fellows should remember and learn from all of this or they could end up being beaned with a bean casserole.

OLDER PRESBYTERIAN WOMEN BELIEVE

- ❑ that no one should be in the express line with more than ten items.
- ❑ that fools' names and fools' faces always appear in public places.
- ❑ that their next husband will be normal.
- ❑ that brag is a good dog.*
- ❑ in the wisdom of Marie Antoinette, who said she didn't care what people did as long as they didn't do it in the streets and frighten the horses!

WE CAN NEVER GO BACK TO BEFORE

In past times, gender roles were clearer. Dad worked and Mom nurtured. In modern times, we seemed to have lost much of that old horizontal and vertical hold. It's for the best.

In the steady but slow progress since they obtained the vote in 1920, women pursued all of the wondrous possibilities of life in that century. By all accounts, they became more educated, more aggressive, and more independent than dependent.

In the 1940s they served our country with distinction in World War II, in the services as well as on the home front. For many, it was the first time they had held a job, and Rosie the Riveter became an international symbol of American patriotism.

In the '60s, protests were staged and laws were passed and governmental policies were developed, all of which helped foster more equality in the workplace. Politicians began to pay more attention to the issues that were traditionally identified with women—education, health

---

*although no one knows quite what this means.

care, and childcare. Today, some soccer moms work for companies that offer flextime and maternity leave—for Dad, too—which go a long way toward enhancing the lives of working women. Even some guys have come around and would maybe support a woman for president, 'cause they joke that she probably still wouldn't have to be paid as much.

Some moms, however, prefer—and can afford—to stay at home to avoid the consequences of jobs—stress and the lack of family time—and thus earn the degree BBA (Bachelor of Baby Administration). Those with more than one child at home intuitively identify with novelist Faye Weldon's reminder that "once you have children, you understand how wars start."

So some moms try to incorporate some religious instruction and prayer in the daily life of their kids. But many learn that they have to say "Amen" twice, because no one listens to you if you just say it once.

Others have no choice. It takes two incomes nowadays to support a family. And many single mothers, in particular, have had to go to work. Some have discovered a new self-esteem in making their own decisions.

Still other young women forego family life and babies for a successful career—big time! But they sometimes find that they are caught in a situation where they are in a double bind. If they are competent, they are often viewed as unfeminine and if they are feminine they are sometimes viewed as incompetent.

Society's changes have involved—and have sometimes been led by—the multitasking women of the Presbyterian church. They are actively engaged in pushing forward, at work and at home, to exciting frontiers with spirit and resolve, even though they often find that they are working at two different demanding jobs. Arlie Hochschild popularized the dual roles of work and family as the *Second Shift* in her book of the same title. And Professor Bonnie J. Miller-Mclemore, writing in *Horizons* (the bimonthly magazine published by Presbyterian Women), questioned whether "having it all" really means "doing it all."

Many of the women in the church, of course, serve the denomination in part- or full-time positions. Others find success in a rainbow of other roles.

But women's overall progress has again raised some questions about gender equality. Are there male/female roles? Who brings home the bacon and who cooks it? Do biological differences count? How much do the cultural, educational, and religious environments contribute to any differences between the sexes? Are men and women more alike than different? Are there REALLY any differences at all?

Such questions have been asked since biblical times. And today, many Presbyterian guys are caught somewhere in the middle of all this, confused by what writer Peggy Kaye calls "the push to be macho men and the pull to be sensitive souls." And there has been a bit of a backlash in the post-feminist world where a few guys feel like the male birds that stop singing when they lose their territory.

Some older fellows in the church sigh and wish for a return to the old days of their fathers and grandfathers, or at least to have the whole thing go away to be somehow settled in the future by somebody else. Some of our female members reportedly feel that way too. They distance themselves from the feminist's joke that if there are hymns there ought to be hers and say that they are feminists but "not one of those radical ones."

And one playful woman notes that just because women go to the ladies' room together, that doesn't mean they all agree on everything.

As Gloria Steinem once quipped, "We're lucky this is the woman's movement. In other movements, they shoot each other."

But most everybody in the church—men and women—DO agree with that affirmative message by the songstress featured in the 1998 Broadway musical *Ragtime*. She offered the sound advice that "we can never go back to before."

We should all learn to embrace that message with Christian love, for the glory and future of all God's children—men and women—here on earth. For as Helen Keller once observed, "I thank God for making woman foolish, so She might be a suitable companion for Man."

PERCY T. PRESBY'S DISCOVERY ABOUT WOMEN'S CLOTHING

Presbyterian working women seem to intuitively understand that a little bit of nothing is vastly more entrancing than nothing at all, but they should probably not try this theory out at their job—or at worship services.

THE CALVINIST FLIP

Many a Victorian mother had the foresight to cover the legs of the grand piano with muslin, so that any young swain who came to call on her daughter wouldn't be moved to licentious thoughts. But it was an elderly Presbyterian matron who came up with the barely discernible little gesture that all skirt-wearing women use to cover their knees when they sit down and cross their legs. According to Percy T. Presby, she first did the wee-bit-of-a-flip on May 16, 1919, just after the Great War, when the new short skirts began to mount an onslaught against that era's modesty.

The same lady is said to have taught her daughters how to arrange their bodies into the Graceful S when they alight, and the proper way to balance a teacup, saucer, and cucumber sandwich.

Some of the older critics have sniffed that she was probably too partial to dresses in plaid that didn't even look good in the shoppe. The pattern was reportedly so Scottish that when she sat down on the couch in her own living room, she lost herself.

Her defenders, however, are legion, and the practices she introduced and the style she created are revered among many of the older women of our church. Rumor has it that she was the grandmother of Martha Stewart, but her true name has been lost in a mist of lavender. In her memory, her supporters supposedly genuflect in an Episcopalian way whenever they pass any fabric or dress shop.

Women don't wear skirts as much anymore. Recently one little girl was heard to question her grandma, "Have you ever worn a dress?" But still today, when Presbyterian women aren't wearing pants, they continue to flip the hems of their skirts when they sit down. If you're a female, don't bother to practice. This gracious little gesture should be automatic.

CHAPEAUX

Women's hats are dead accessories. But time was when a Presbyterian matron wouldn't attend church without something perched on her head.

She had bought into a culture that was established by Eve and endorsed by Paul's first letter to the Corinthians (chapter 11:13–15) in which he set out the rules for hair— short for men and long for women. And later, the longer length seemed to almost demand the use of a hat to REALLY act as a covering when praying and to sorta' top things off.

The accessory was often green or pink, made of tulle, straw, or felt, and had a wide brim. Some were simple little pillboxes. Others were as big as a car and had to be anchored down with hatpins. A beautiful few had ostrich feathers. Sometimes, the lady's shoes were dyed to match the object on her head.

At Eastertide, the sanctuary was a sea of bobbing bonnets, as all the female folk welcomed spring with a rainbow of colors! At the coffee hour, they exclaimed over one another's choice: "Delightful!" and "Charming!" were some of the accolades. Only a few were dismissed with that faint praise, "Interesting!"

Writer Alison Lurie once said that "whatever is worn on the head is a sign of the mind beneath it." That didn't appear to be so for many of our females, who seemed to believe that whatever was on their heads could temporarily change their character, thus creating an illusion within as well as without.

Every Sunday, however, lots of Presbyterian guys stood around in a forest of cheerful color, beaming. Alas, hats are pretty much gone now, so our members who are women don't usually have to worry about which one to wear to church. A lot of the fellows say that's a pity, but you can't go back to before.

PERCY T. PRESBY'S OBSERVATION ABOUT FEMALE JOBS

To many Presbyterian women, what they don't do is as important as what they do do.

HANDBAGS

When you first attended a Presbyterian church, you undoubtedly noticed the ladies' purses. Some folks say that they seem to be bigger than other women's.

For many of our matrons, their carryalls have hung on their shoulders so long they seem to have become permanent appendages. On some of the older members, the accumulated weight over the years has given them a noticeable list to one side when they walk down the aisle.

The single young ladies of today don't seem to be burdened with such large containers. But as they marry, the size of the bag grows in direct relationship to the number of children they have. What starts out as a modest handbag gradually takes on the proportion of a small suitcase.

The things become portable candy, drug, and hardware stores, and apparently the receptacle of all of a woman's worldly possessions. Folks say that if a tornado ever destroys their town, by golly, these women are ready!

For out of them comes an incredible number of life's just-in-case necessities: keys, safety pins, needles, thread, toys, bandages, candy, rubber bands, aspirin, scissors, shoelaces, pencils, paper clips, tape measures, moisturizers—and a wallet that is bigger than any man's.

The contents seem to change and increase as the children grow older. Interred then are library cards, note pads, watches, timetables, school schedules, shopping lists, bank deposit slips, cough drops, rain bonnets, PTA minutes, dental appointments, sun glasses, and a growing assortment of cosmetics.

To see some of the women of our church rummage through the interior of a bag looking for their offering envelope during a Sunday service is like watching a dog dig for a bone. There are often some things they find that even they didn't know were there. Like a church bulletin from last August!

The handbags are replaced periodically according to some unfathomable (to the male) timetable. If a fella' watches closely over the months, a new one of a different color and heft will probably appear on various shoulders in some sort of mysterious but coordinated ballet. The discarded ones presumably go off to Pocketbook Heaven.

The autocratic former British Prime Minister, Margaret Thatcher, made her handbags a symbol of her authority and contributed a new word to the English language. British politicians were said to be "handbagged" by her, for her seemingly bottomless carryalls were filled with intimidating objects and statements that supported her arguments. And the term has now been memorialized in the Oxford English Dictionary:

To Handbag: transitive verb (of a woman politician), to treat (a person, idea etc.) ruthlessly or insensitively.

To many an English politician, the Prime Minister's handbags were both feared and worshipped and thus served as a potent reminder of her sex.

Today, if you're a woman in the United States, all you have to do is to step up to the next handbag size when you join the Presbyterian church. If you're a man, stay out of the way of the things. Some have been known to accidentally maim an usher!

PERCY T. PRESBY'S WISDOM ABOUT THE LADIES

Many Presbyterian women never seem to think that rules are made to be broken.

OLDER PRESBYTERIAN WOMEN DON'T

- ❑ use toothpicks.
- ❑ answer the phone on the first ring.
- ❑ trust anybody who does her own hair.
- ❑ wear white to church before Easter or after Labor Day.
- ❑ whistle, because whistling girls and crowing hens always come to some bad end.

OLDER PRESBYTERIAN WOMEN DO

- ❑ play bridge.
- ❑ make tasty potato salad.
- ❑ wear good Republican cloth coats.
- ❑ carry handkerchiefs in their sleeves.
- ❑ understand cats' condescending facial expressions and how to bathe them.

THE PW

The women of our denomination occupy important positions as elders, deacons, and ministers. They are dynamic and influential, finding a balance between their busy weekday life and a vigorous leadership in all aspects of church life. But truth be told, others undertake their many denomination-oriented tasks because, like Ado Annie in *Oklahoma*, they "can't say no."

If you're of the female persuasion, you're hopefully also going to get involved in the Presbyterian Women (PW). They used to be called the United Presbyterian Women (UPW), but Percy T. Presby jokes that someone discovered that there wasn't as much solidarity as they thought, so they dropped the first word. It's now the PW.

Under whatever name, every year this organization is instrumental in planning and running dozens of functions in our churches throughout the land. In addition to holding successful fairs and banquets, retreats and Bible study meetings, the PW is a very informed and influential voice in the future of our church.

Although their membership is declining (because many women are in the daily work force and unable to attend daytime meetings), they initiate and imaginatively manage the important work of our denomination in hundreds of ways. And they joyfully engage in what is called the "Second Mile Giving"—the donation of money that is over and above the regular family/woman pledges to the church.

Some of the older members—those who have seen it all—allow that sometimes the PW folks "do go on." The talk and bustle at their events is said to be quite remarkable. A few of the women are reportedly prone to announce out loud, to no one in particular, the next task they are going to tackle as the activity unfolds. All of these people talking to themselves evidently results in a great deal of noise.

Still, everyone agrees that positive actions do take place—actions that inspire and lead to wonderful benefits within our denomination. There IS a concern about who will provide future leadership in the PW organization. A charming cartoon character, "Searching Sarah," has been created to help address this problem. So when her human counterparts ask you to serve as a leader, please consider it.

Some of the older PW members advise, however, that if you're a man and somehow get involved in one of their sessions, be prepared to fight a sorta' irresistible urge to go watch a ball game and drink a beer the next night with a bunch of guys. Or at least to get together and shave.

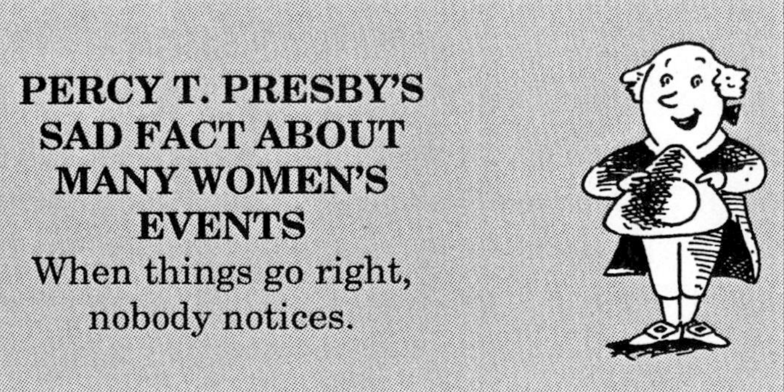

THE FOUR W'S RULE

When you become a member of the PW you're probably going to hear about the old "Presbyterian Potluck Rule." It's also referred to by many as the "Four W's Rule." The ordinance has been in existence now for nearly 60 years, and it's a pretty good thing to adhere to if you're put in charge of a church covered-dish dinner. And you will be. Every PW member draws that duty at some time.

They say the regulation stems from a disastrous incident that happened during World War II in a little Iowa town. It was sort of a potluck dinner that went astray.

For Aunt Ethel (who was in charge) simply forgot to phone people and ask them—or assign them—to bring either a salad or a hot dish or rolls or a dessert to the potluck. And no one noticed!

Each housewife was not particularly concerned when Ethel didn't call. Each one simply figured that she had been inadvertently forgotten, and made her plans to attend anyhow. Each assumed that Ethel had worked out a proper balance between all the salads, hot dishes, rolls, and desserts that everybody was bringing, and that any single contribution wouldn't tip the scale too badly one way or the other. So each cook decided she'd bring what she did best, or what her husband liked, or whatever she felt like making.

The result was that at 12:30 P.M. on Sunday, July 25, 1943, as the members gathered under the shade trees at the church, there were unveiled four Jello salads (with marshmallows on top), two baskets of rolls, four cherry pies; and 21 hot dishes—all of which had baked beans as the primary ingredient!

No one knew quite what to do. The only restaurant—the Cozy Corner—was closed because Flo and Henry were on vacation, trying to catch walleyes at Lake Wanapeg over the state line in Minnesota. The only other place to get salads or any other food on a Sunday was 40 miles away.

So there was nothing for it. The Presbyterian parson said grace, and everyone lined up and began filling up their plates. In the Christian spirit of things, lots of people didn't take any of the rolls or a piece of pie or any of the salads. Others just took a dab or two of those scarce commodities—to be polite, they said. The heavy eaters (and there were many for this was a hardworking farming community) all took what was most available—hearty portions of the seemingly infinite varieties of baked bean casseroles.

When the news of the potluck menu drifted down to the pool hall, where the town loafers had the radio tuned to the St. Louis Cardinals baseball game that Sunday afternoon, there were some whoops and a knee slap or two.

Then some other people from neighboring hamlets picked up the tale and it became the topic of conversation when the farmers came into those towns on the next Saturday night for grocery shopping. And the Baptists and Congregationalist ladies and others who held church potluck dinners began to warn their members about the need for meticulous planning for such events, using the incident as an example of what could happen if one didn't mind her P's and Q's.

But it took our friends the Methodists, to finally put a tag on it in a national magazine for women published by their Women's Society of Christian Service (WSCS). In a long article, the WSCS detailed the correct way to organize a potluck dinner, ending with the strong admonition that one should follow the Four W's Rule to Write down Who is bringing What and When!

They even included a form that could be copied; it had three columns—for Who, What, and When. And in a bit of a dig at their fellow Christians, they titled the sheet "The Presbyterian Potluck Form."

All through the spreading of the tale about the incident, the offices of the Presbyteries and Synods and General Assembly did their best to ignore the many jokes from their brethren from other churches and tongue-in-cheek reports in the media. After all, the event had not been an official church function. And you will find no reference to the Four W's in any Presbyterian church literature, or in the official *Book of Order.*

But you will hear about it whenever Presbyterian men and women gather to eat a communal dinner. It's wise to remember the rule by putting up the form or a similar one by your telephone or on your refrigerator door whenever you're in charge of one of those potluck affairs. Though Aunt Ethel's dead now, she would certainly have appreciated it, for she was a Christian woman who hoped others would profit from her mistakes in life.

PERCY T. PRESBY'S PROBABILITY ABOUT POTLUCKS

A Presbyterian woman will never bring pickled herring to a potluck dinner, and will refuse to use egg whites in her salad, because she remembers reading somewhere that Casanova said that both were aphrodisiacs.

PRESBYTERIAN WOMEN GET CRANKY WHEN

- ❑ a guy leaves a white ring from a hot cup of coffee on a walnut table in the church parlor.
- ❑ the Catholic ladies from the Church of the Immaculate Kitchen win most of the blue ribbons at the county fair.
- ❑ some guy defines sexual harassment.

- ❑ the Lutheran ladies' bowling team swipes the name "Holy Rollers" that their Sarah Circle has been using for its baking group.
- ❑ a president lies to them.

PERCY T. PRESBY'S OBSERVATION ABOUT PRESBYTERIAN WOMEN

A lot of the female persons in the church appear to have been taught from childhood to roll their eyes, particularly when some dopey guy is trying to explain tanks to them.

THE MEN WHO LOVE WOMEN

Younger guys in our denomination don't seem to have many problems dealing with members of the opposite sex. It's a bit harder for us senior fellows. In addition to respecting the manifold contributions made to church life by these members, many older Presbyterian men revere the many other aspects of the female persons. Included in this admiration is a regard for their blend of pride and vulnerability and their civilizing and loving presence.

Many of we Frozen Chosen fellows have always been slaves to the female, both individually and collectively. Some observers claim that we have worshipped and adored them for more than 400 years, silently acknowledging deep within ourselves that women are God's superior product. In spite of John Knox, many venerable Calvinist men have always believed that the female is fundamentally the most marvelous of the sexes, full of continuous delights and glorious sunrises.

While recognizing their skills and talents, we are still enamored of the ladies in the "Red Silk Stockings and the Green Perfume," as the old song goes. And some of us can fondly remember the hours profitably spent "standing on the corner, watching all the girls go by."

But men look at the ideal, women at the real. Some of us ancients have elevated the female to such a lofty position that it's almost impossible for them to live up to it. Anyhow, as Congresswoman Patsy Mink once quipped, the female's natural superiority makes it difficult for them to lower themselves far enough to become the equal of men. We older Presbyterian fellows regret that this generation seems to have brought women down to the level of men, which is a terrible price to pay for equality according to some. They reason that women who want to be equal to men lack ambition.

For no less of a feminist than Lady Violet Bonham Carter came to the conclusion that there are only three occupations in which men will always have the edge: hairdressing, dressmaking, and cooking.

We timeworn Presbyterian fellows continue to idealize the female, forgetting that insightful remark made by Barbara Stanwyck. She told Henry Fonda in the 1941 movie, *The Lady Eve*, "You don't know very much about girls, Hopsie. The best ones aren't as good as you probably think they are, and the bad ones aren't nearly as bad!"

But our respect and admiration for the persons of the opposite sex is seldom overt. The Presbyterian older fella' doesn't usually praise the successful summer Bible School that was organized and run by the women on the Christian Education Committee. Nor does he publicly commend the scholarly leadership in a class on church history by an elder who happens to be a woman.

And he usually doesn't stare open-mouthed at a new hairdo or dress or sniff appreciably at some perfume. Nor does he gaze wonderingly at her breathless touch of evening and promised gift of springtime. Self-restraint is the ticket.

In fact, he usually acts like an unromantic clod who should never be left unsupervised and is best kept outdoors. For the old guy is prone to give his wife two steel-belted radial tires for Valentine's Day, signing the card "Cordially." It all leaves some of the 58 percent of our denomination who are women muttering that if we can send one man to the moon, we ought to able to send ALL of them there—or at least be able to get rid of ESPN.

And some women now interpret Revelations 9:32 ("When hairless Goliaths bestride the earth, woe be unto thee who gather at their squared circle to worship graven images") as a comment about that dreadful hobby of the men who go to World Wide Wrestling Federation matches. And as a dire warning that the apocalypse is just about upon us.

But in spite of it all, for some of us old-timers, the love and respect for the women of our church doesn't go away. It's there when one adroitly manages a consensus at a spirited committee meeting. And it's there when she brushes her hair behind her ear, and in her smile that's as beautiful and quiet as a bird on the wing.

Sometimes, some of us older guys go too far and develop an unspoken hankering to love every woman in our denomination between 21 and too-old. While those few seek to become industrial-strength sinners, most of us simply want to lie down in front of a fireplace and have our bellies rubbed by our wives.

A lot of us have learned by now not to bring flowers home to those wives on an impulse. All we may get is a suspicious look. And it is finally clear to us that if a man is talking in the forest and no woman is there to hear him, he is still wrong.

But they say that it's normal for some of us older Presbyterian fellows to want to spend part of our summer vacation as one of the few male delegates among the lively 5,000 ladies at the Triennial Presbyterian Women's Convention. Known as "the Gathering," it appears to be a place where the ladies fair let down their hair, to borrow a phrase from Dr. Lewis Thomas. And it happens every three years.

Relating to the women members in our church seemingly poses no problem for the younger guys in our denomination. Their attitude and relationship with the opposite sex is more sanguine, so they don't have to be concerned about all of this. Perhaps that will change however, as they grow in years.

For there is no end to the rainbow of love for the female for some older Presbyterian men. You should understand that's just the way it is. If you're a lady, ignore our stupidities and please—smile back more often.

God wants you to!

PERCY T. PRESBY'S THOUGHTS ON THE PARADOX OF THE FEMALE

It IS difficult for some Presbyterian men of any age to understand how the wonderful complexity that is woman can attend the I-Hate-My-Hair self-exploration seminar at the Women's Center in the church one week, and be back for the one on Sexual Harassment the next week, and so they finally agree that they "just don't get it."

ONE DIFFERENCE

There ARE some manifold differences between men and women. One of them is undeniable. Some 1,800 greeting card makers in the United States are funded in large part by female expectations. There are all sorts of holidays, events, and happenings that require a modern *billet doux.* And surveys indicate that women purchase more than 80 percent of all cards.

But for most males, buying a card is an unnatural act. And it's most often done at the last moment. The columnist Bob Weimen says that in the Roman Catholic church, Valentines Day is a male Day of Obligation. So it is with us Presbyterian men. Please be tolerant. We're trying.

PERCY T. PRESBY'S MUSINGS ABOUT FEMALE PERSONS

To many Presbyterian males, the REAL mystery of the female is that she doesn't think there IS any mystery, for after all, the thinnest book in the world is titled *What Men Know About Women.*

UNDERSTANDINGS

Presbyterian women are said to understand (1) the difference between ecru, off-white, and eggshell; (2) the inaccuracy of every bathroom scale ever made; and (3) other women.

PRESBYTERIAN NUTRITION

If you are a guest in another member's home, you will discover that some old time Presbyterian cooks follow the "Mabel Hammer School of Cuisine" when it comes to nourishment. Hammer was the Julia Child of South Dakota.

She was also the home economics teacher at the high school in Wolsey, South Dakota (population 297), where her most popular course was "How to Boil Water!" It had an enrollment of five—all boys. She was also the wife of the editor of the *Wolsey News*, and the organist for the First Presbyterian Church.

In school, she taught her charges that every meal should be balanced by color. Under her scheme, one should have yellows, reds, browns, and greens for a wholesome meal. A nutritious repast might consist of well-done beef (brown), corn (yellow), and lettuce (green), topped off by a cherry pie (red).

Folks thereabouts say that for that reason, only the most courageous Presbyterian cooks have two dishes of the same color in any meal. This explains some of the odd combinations of food you may encounter when dining at an older member's house in South Dakota. And Mrs. Hammer's influence is said to have spread throughout the United States.

You might want to watch out for this when you are a dinner guest at another member's home. It's another of the wondrous phenomena in our church and further proof that our cups runneth over.

PERCY T. PRESBY'S DEFINITION OF A PRESBYTERIAN MAN

A Presbyterian male is one who, after pondering the biblical passage about "an eye for an eye and a tooth for a tooth," will conclude that he should begin to collect discarded glasses and used dentures to give to the Lion's Club for distribution to the needy.

GRIP AND GRAB

According to most accounts, handshakes were started as a way of showing that neither guy was carrying a weapon. They then turned into a gesture that sealed an agreement and finally into a friendly greeting.

And it would appear that there is a Presbyterian handshake. If you're a man, you'd better learn it, for it's used on many church occasions.

The actual grasp is neither wimpish nor a massive crunching of another's bones. It's just a sort of bland, nondescript clutching of someone's hand. It's easy and should come rather naturally.

The motion is another matter. Timing is important. You are not supposed to employ the one-jerk wrench favored by European women.

Neither do you use the 24-pump version used by some American crop insurance salesmen.

Nope, you go for the two-up-and-down rendition, which signifies earnest but dignified human contact. If you're misty-eyed over something that the person has done, or if you haven't seen him in 20 years, you are supposedly allowed to raise your arm up and down three times.

In church, the handshake is sometimes used during or after the Sunday service to greet others. And everybody lines up to gently squeeze the hand of the preacher on their way out. This ritual hopefully satisfies two needs.

From the ministers' standpoint, it allows them to receive at least some recognition for their hard work that morning, even if it only takes the form of a mumbled "nice sermon." It also allows the parsons to surreptitiously take attendance and chat up potential members.

From your viewpoint as a member, the hand contact is a chance to remind the clergyperson that you were present that morning, and that you hope that fact will be remembered to God the next time the two of them have a prayerful conversation. ("By the way, Lord…")

So you should try to brush up on the warm Presbyterian grip and motion. It's yet another part of God's good grace here on earth!

GO FOR IT!

Men should probably be aware that their fellow male church members are sometimes masochists when it comes to sports. They often seek out those that give them the opportunity to enjoy the thrill of agony and the victory of defeat. Like Chicago Cubs fans, they start talking about the prospects for "next season" during spring training for THIS season.

Only a few of us take it into our heads, however, that we are true sportsmen. We reportedly go for individual rather than team sports, having learned at church committee meetings not to place too much trust in our fellow man.

Cross-country skiing, snowmobiling, and an occasional jog in the twilight seem to suit the solitary member who wants only himself to lose to. Outsiders say that if we genial Presbyterians are feeling particularly competitive, there is always croquet—as long as it's not too fierce a match. They claim a spirited round of pickup sticks can also get our blood boiling,

Golf, however, seems to fit the bill best for the men in the denomination, even though Mark Twain called it "a good walk spoiled." In addition to having been invented in Scotland, the game offers us the opportunity to agonize over lost balls and to celebrate the defeat by standing for the losers' round of refreshments at the nineteenth hole. Some Presbyterian ministers even reportedly belong to the PGA (Preachers Golf Association).

Losing, of course, is preordained. God wants us to suffer while at play. Occasionally some of the younger fellows may embrace that philosophy with a vengeance by forming a basketball team to play in a church league. If you have ever had any game experience past high school, you may be called upon to coach.

You will be going up against the Methodist Marauders, the Catholic Crusaders, and the Baptist Bombers, among others. Prepare yourself for some humiliating defeats with your—what else?—Presbyterian Pumpkins.

Not to worry. One season of basketball losses should be enough to drive you and everyone else back to some individual pastimes. But keep in mind, Presbyterians usually don't bowl.*

---

*Some do! In 1996, Pastor C. K. Moore, then at Snohomish, Washington, joined the PBA tour and became Rookie of the Year!

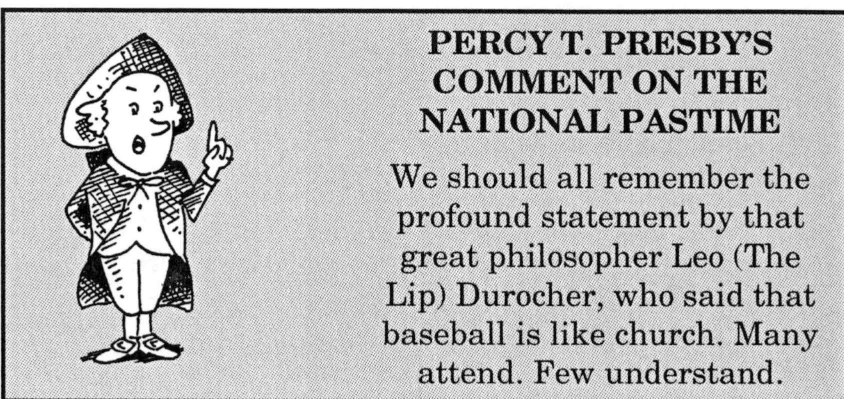

POM POMS AND PIGTAILS

After a fella' joins the denomination, he will make the discovery that every fourth junior high school cheerleader in the United States is a Presbyterian kid. It's one of the few church secrets kept from outsiders, says Percy T. Presby.

The button-nosed youngsters jump, squeal, and do cartwheels in occasional synchronization. They have braces and white shoes and short pleated skirts and an enormous amount of pep. They also hug a lot.

While they don't do their thing at church functions, you will not be able to escape them in the secular world. Not that you'll want to. They're full of spunk and pluck and life. You should try not to tug a pigtail when they go by.

TOMORROW ARRIVED THIS MORNING

Although it's popular these days to talk of the female menopause, some men are vulnerable to a similar middle-aged malady—the Male

Menopause. Presbyterian guys are not immune. The thing creeps up on them in the afternoon of their life sometime after they turn 40. And it's pretty bad—particularly the Presbyterian version.

For it's an intensely internal indisposition, which is a curious blend of ennui and angst, creating tidal surges of emotion and a mad muddle of the mind. It acts like the thirteenth stroke of a clock, bringing up questions about all that precedes and follows it.

To combat the contagion, some guys resort to the bottle, seeking to make beer the fifth food group. They seem to care to remember, but drink to forget. Others flee to a psychiatrist's couch. One or two have been known to seek help from their Presbyterian minister—which is okay unless he's going through the same thing himself.

Guys at the midlife crisis find their politics are changing. They are beginning to understand the wisdom of former presidential candidate Wendell Wilkie, who came up with the notion that "any man who is not something of a socialist before he is 40 has no heart, and any man who is still something of a socialist after he is 40, has no head." They are finding that the older they get, the more conservative they become.

These baby boomers grew up thinking that Mary Tyler Moore was Mary Richards, not Laura Petrie, and they can sing all the opening lyrics to the *Brady Bunch* theme song by heart. They had mood rings, lava lamps, and pet rocks and listened to the Allman Brothers and the Rolling Stones. But even back then the typical church member was never really an MCP (Male Chauvinist Presbyterian) for he certainly saw the righteousness of equal pay and the unfairness of much of the treatment of the opposite sex.

But he did get confused by some of the extremely militant feminists who seemed to blame every ill of humanity on men and spent a lot of time bashing the boys in the gender wars. He never did really buy the idea that all men are Neanderthals on parole from the Museum of Natural History, who rise burping from the restaurant table and lunge for the nearest waitress growling, "Now, me have fun!"

And over the years, he has finally learned that men and women often use language differently, and his consciousness has been raised so that he can sometimes walk in Her shoes. And then along came the issue of sexual harassment. There were two ways to pronounce it, and at least 2200 ways to define it.

This has created all sorts of confusion and a predictable rush to take things to some extremes in the sexual war zone. And male casualties have been pretty heavy. One aged university faculty member was officially reprimanded for committing "offensive staring" through his goggles at an elderly female colleague in the swimming pool.

The Presbyterian menopausal male is confused, of course, about his emotions and relationships. So he continues to snuggle up to his loving wife

It quite often takes two incomes now to keep the family going, and the menopausal male is not sure how that happened. His warm and delectable spouse has become an important career person and full of contradictions. She calls the tenth inning of a World Series game "overtime" and then gets that "I-Know-That-Was-Dumb-But-I'm-Only-a-Girl-and-You-Love-Me-Anyway-'Cause-I'm-Cute" look on her face. The next morning she goes into her workplace and fires somebody!

He and his partner have raised their kids in the Nike era, where the cost of that American icon is enough to pay for a semester's college tuition in the old days. And they have long since become inured to their bleeding-from-the-ears hip-hop music that's so loud that the folks on Mars can hear it.

Some of the befuddled guys spent some time trying to hand out advice when their kids were growing up, but although they chopped a lot, few chips fell. About the only thing that is reported to have stuck was their warning that the kids shouldn't let their mom comb their hair when she was mad at their dad!

So the Presbyterian menopausal male spends a lot of his time being shown hard things and drinking of the "wine of astonishment," to quote the Psalmist David. For he has become persuaded that God probably has a particularly antic sense of humor when it comes to modern life.

How else to explain gambling in Iowa, for heaven's sake, or Presbyterians who play "The Green Parrot Polka" on the accordion on public television in rural Pennsylvania. And when it comes to health insurance, some folks keep telling him that Jesus had to be born in a stable because his parents belonged to a predecessor of an HMO. He is also beginning to believe that he has lived too long when he hears a rumor that the Girl Scouts are handing out merit badges for stress management, and among all the profusion of catalogs in the mail, he receives a brochure offering to sell him a Three Stooges Christmas Ornament Set for only $13.95.

He has to suck in his stomach and grope his way through many get-togethers nowadays, for he keeps meeting good-natured, warmhearted people whose elevator seems to have missed a few floors on its way to the top. Some of them are truly a piece of work, making it sometimes difficult to follow that admonishment in Roman's 15:17 that you should "accept one another, as Christ has accepted you, in order to bring praise to God."

For by the door is an amiable doofus with a sort of Floyd-of-Mayberry haircut who teaches canaries to sing for a living. He's just got a degree in some discipline that's so arcane he has stopped trying to explain it to people. There's sometimes a gentle hardware clerk who is terribly optimistic and has just invented something he calls "A Thousand and One Islands Dressing." Its introduction into the market will require a giant leap of faith, and he wants your support—financially.

And over by the window is a neighborly farmer who is also an engaging and playful political artist. He says he makes snowballs in the winter and as a protest against capital punishment, he signs them on street corners in the nearby city.

As a Presbyterian, the menopausal male knows he's supposed to cherish them—oddities not withstanding. They are, he keeps saying to himself, living examples that God loves all of the brothers and sisters in our church family.

And although he's come to accept Presbyterian euphemisms as a necessary part of life in the modern denomination, he is becoming somewhat annoyed at them in daily life. These days, hallways are apparently *behavior transition corridors*, swamps are *wetlands*, folks that won't laugh are the *humorously challenged,* and older people are the *chronologically gifted*, according to the politically correct police.

He has also noted with some concern that the Harvard Divinity School is so racially sensitive that they changed the word for their recycling bins from *colored paper* to *paper of color* and finally to *dyed paper.*

Many guys just give up, sigh, and identify with that melancholy country western song, "Much Too Young (to Feel This Damn Old)."

But if you are going through this thing, it's wise to remember that the whole male menopausal hassle has been going on for centuries. You are not boldly going where no man has gone before.

In your anguish, you may attempt to connect all the philosophical dots. Some of our fellows grow beards, put leather patches on their elbows, pick up a pipe, and sign up for New Age courses like "Riding the Tiger of Crazy Wisdom," taught by an "ethnopharmacologist and psychedelic theoretician." Some turn Catholic so they can see the Virgin Mary's face in the bathroom of an auto parts store in Progresso, Texas. And some in Michigan just sit in front of the television tube getting misty-eyed over reruns of *The Wonder Years*. The Portuguese have a word for that—*saudades*—which denotes a nostalgia for something that may never have existed.

A few abandon everything and retreat to Resume Speed, Arizona or Piquot, Ohio—home of the Great Outdoor Underwear Festival—every October.

Many are reportedly torn between feeling guilty about something they did when they were nine years old and their unspoken, never-to-be-realized fantasy to host a party with ten floozies wearing nine costumes, swinging from the chandeliers.

The guilt will go, with some help from a sympathetic wife and perhaps a minister friend. For as sports columnist Jan Hubbard reminds us, so far as anyone knows, there was only one perfect Man.

So as you lurch forward in this new traffic jam in your life, relax and take comfort in the realization that you have many wondrous adventures awaiting you before you dance off to that weightless Presbyterian city in the sky. Remember that after the Middle Ages came the Renaissance. And for those who would hold back the dawn for you, remind them that tomorrow arrived this morning!

WATCH IT!

Along with middle age come various ailments. Among them is something called *presbyopia*. Although it really has nothing to do with our denomination, some optometrists say that the blurred vision that creates a need for glasses after age 40 particularly affects the male members of our church. Something about synergy.

A YEA FOR MODESTY

As a male, you may occasionally do something praiseworthy during your life in the church. So you should learn to accept congratulations in the Presbyterian way, which is to say with great modesty and a quiet acceptance of any accolades that may come your way.

Not for you are fists punching the air or two arms held aloft in triumph. There should be no boogying down as if you had just scored a touchdown. Even a bow is probably a bit much.

No, you should learn to adopt the posture that your superior performance is so commonplace that it doesn't merit much attention—least of all from you. That it is instantly recognized is a given. But you must treat applause as the most ordinary thing and your accomplishment as being so routine that you seem to be casually tossing the ball to the official in the end zone after a 98-yard run. This is, of course, in tune with that sanguine philosophy of old Princeton coaches, who traditionally taught their charges that when a gentleman scores a touchdown he should act like he's done it before and expects to do it again!

You are permitted to acknowledge any tributes with a nod. But not more than one. They say that would be shameless.

To compensate, it's different in the outside world. Today, if you are being praised and touted for a triumph by your fellow workers, you are free to strut up and down with a massive grin on your face, giving high fives and shouting "YESSSS!" Fair's fair.

PERCY T. PRESBY'S ANTIDOTE FOR A TOUGH DAY AT THE CHURCH

According to bartenders, a Presbyterian is made of rye, ginger ale, and club soda.

WHEELS

From time to time during your church membership you will probably be in the position of buying a new car. According to the polls, going shopping for a new car is right up there with the things Americans most dread. Like going to the dentist, there's always a feeling of being violated somehow!

The salesperson seems to know more than you do about the insides of the thing, and always has to check with the boss before responding to your little counteroffer. You suspect you're being taken and you feel helpless to do anything about it.

And you're expected to do a very un-Presbyterian thing—bargain. Haggling over money is usually foreign to most church members.

The real problem, though, is what kind of a car to set out to buy in the first place. There are more than 134 types of them on the road today, many made by the Japanese. A lot of them seem to be named after different kinds of pantyhose, like *Sundance* and *Caprice*.

Time was when there were only Chevys and Plymouths and Fords and the like, and you usually bought what your dad or granddad had owned. They never went for newfangled transportation like the Kaiser, the Frazer, or the Tucker Torpedo. And they certainly never bought a Japanese made vehicle, having been taught all the lyrics to "Remember Pearl Harbor."

There are ways, however, that you can narrow today's many choices down. Some say that religious membership and car ownership are inexorably entwined—as long as you "Buy American."

According to Percy T. Presby, the Jewish folk usually buy Cadillacs, Episcopalians opt for Lincoln Town Cars, and United Church of Christ members go for Pontiacs. The Lutherans have a yen for Plymouth sedans, and the Baptists are partial to good solid Chevys. The Methodists have always favored four-door Fords, but no one has ever been able to pinpoint exactly what the members of our friends in the Catholic church buy in the way of cars. Some jokers say, however, that any such purchase must be approved by the Pope.

The Presbyterians, of course, choose Oldsmobiles, according to the Percy T. Presby. They are a sort of staid means of transportation that make a restrained, yet positive, statement by being somewhat (but not too) large and expensive.

So the merry Olds it is, from the "Good Old, Good Olds Guys." You'll probably have a problem, however, finding a fellow member to sell one to you. There seem to be very few car salespeople who are of the Frozen Chosen. The Calvinist personality just doesn't know how to "open" let alone "close" a deal.

(Some of your fellow members do serve in sales in retail stores because people have to come to them and request something. Some are even spurred to tentatively ask, "May I help you?" But high-pressure sales tactics, like high blood pressure, are usually avoided by your wonderful new friends in the church.)

So you're pretty much on your own out there on the highway near the mall at Charlie's Oldsmobile Emporium. Good luck!

COLOR ME…

When you do buy your new Oldsmobile, you'll have to choose a color. It should be a good Presbyterian one. Red, of course, is out. Statistically, red cars are given more tickets than any other car on the road. And black as the ultimate power color is also a no-no.

Yellow is too artistic and the very popular silver will make the vehicle look like a jewelry accessory. And any of those offbeat colors on the cars that are sold to Floridians probably won't look good in the rest of the country.

Green is said to be too socially conscious and romantic, and white is too cautious and bland even though it's now popular. So you're left with conservative gray, brown, or the blue, each of which denote consistency. And the advice from here is—go for the blue!

According to color consultants, it's the hue of an introvert or maybe an extrovert who likes to be able to count on certain things. Author Marina Warner says it's the color of both desire and melancholy, the marvelous and the inexplicable. What could be more Presbyterian?

"True Blue" was originally "Presbyterian True Blue" and blue is sorta' the unofficial church color. Go for it!

NO SWEAT LEADERSHIP

If you are a man, you'll maybe find yourself in charge of the Property and Maintenance Committee at some time during your membership in the church. Although the church is officially nonsexist, many members are said to somehow feel a bit more at ease when a male is in charge of repaving the parking lot or repairing the front steps of the sanctuary.

The maintenance job is sort of a practical, take-charge assignment. There is, therefore, a temptation here, particularly if you have ever served in the military at any time.

If you are a veteran, you are advised to curb your instincts and keep old Army/Navy jargon out of your vocabulary. Your fellow members are peace-loving folk who don't take kindly to orders of any kind. We Presbyterians normally ease into a course of action in a sideways, crab-like manner, and by the dint of a sort of consensus of the spirit—"if the way be clear!"

Men and women volunteers of all ages will arrive to help with the annual church cleanup and work day. This is not the time to divide them into squads and platoons. There should be no drillling with rakes and shovels in the parking lot before attacking the shrubbery.

You should probably also refrain from calling rest breaks and advising them that they can "smoke 'em if ya' got 'em." You should also not direct the associate pastor to "Belay that!" or to "move the troops out of the hot sun." And under no circumstance should you pipe the pastor aboard the dump truck with your buddy's old bosun's pipe.

But you won't need me to tell you all of this. You'll know it yourself when members of the Peacemaking Committee start to picket your house carrying placards saying "Yankee Go Home" and singing "We Shall Overcome." An experience like that is often instructive and will truly help you move forward in your refurbishing of the image of our new church!

DOMESTICITY

When putting the dishes in the dishwasher the traditional Presbyterian male somehow manages to convey the impression that he did all the cooking. But he never empties the thing and puts the dishes away.

Today in some of our churches, the men are doing much of the cooking for all-member events. You guys should try to remember that we should carry this type of contribution home more often, if we want to obtain the Good Husband Seal of Approval.

YOU MADE IT!

You'll know you've become a full-fledged Presbyterian person when you acquire the characteristic described by that unpronounceable Scottish word, *sgiomlaireachd* ("the habit of dropping in at mealtimes"). And as a female, you no longer have a yen for salads and as a man you are no longer feeling carnivorous. And both of you have developed a great hankering for potluck dinners in Fellowship Hall.

Chapter Six

DAILY LIFE

PERCY T. PRESBY'S OBSERVATION ABOUT PRESBYTERIAN FAMILIES

Presbyterians live in a sort of genteel family coziness; Roseanne and her TV clan were never members of our church.

THE GOOD LIFE

Observers have said that that we Presbyterians are usually not very adventuresome in our civilian life. It just won't do. We like an existence that is comfortable enough to wrap up in like a warm blanket and a place where, they say, even the moonlight tiptoes.

We follow the Greek model, *megan agen*—nothing in excess. Not for us are the tavern-crawling nights of abandoned dancing or cruises to exotic climes. We instead find contentment in sunny summer picnics under the trees or with a hot chocolate and our family in front of the fireplace on a snowy winter night.

But by now, you've discovered all this. Isn't it great?

PERCY T. PRESBY'S MUSINGS ON COMMUTING

The millennium reminded us that the sudden switch from BC to AD after the birth of Jesus must have caused a lot of people to miss their camel ride to work.

NAME DROPPING

You are, of course, allowed to insert the names of the denomination's famous members into your workday conversations. There have been a bunch of them, but in modest Presbyterian fashion, most such worthy members didn't—and don't—advertise their membership. But the Presbyterians have supplied the nation with some of its grandest personalities.

Twelve of the signers of the Declaration of Independence were Presbyterians and one—John Witherspoon—was an ordained minister. And there have been a bunch of U.S. presidents, including James Polk and James Buchanan. And the Great Emancipator himself, Abraham Lincoln, attended our church. Presidents Grover Cleveland and Benjamin Harrison were members, and of course, idealist Woodrow Wilson. Some famous Civil War generals were also Presbyterians, including Stonewall Jackson. And in World War II, Presbyterian Dwight David Eisenhower won the battle of Europe. Running on what some said was a platform of incomplete sentences, he became president in the placid 1950s, presiding over what still others called the "Presbyterian Decade."

Former astronaut (and former Senator) John Glenn is an active member of the church, and then there's ex-Vice President Dan Quayle. He's a Presbyterian, as was his former boss, Ronald Reagan. And former President George Bush was once an active deacon and elder.

In the literary world there was author Pearl Buck, winner of the Nobel Peace Prize, and the Presbyterian missionary Reverend William McGuffey whose *Readers* made America literate in the 1800s. Henry Luce, who founded *Time* magazine, and Dewitt Wallace, who started *The Readers Digest*, were sons of Presbyterian ministers.

The nation's greatest orator of the 19th century, William Jennings Bryan, was a member of the church. Not surprisingly, Gilbert Grosvenor, founder of the National Geographic Society and its magazine, was a Presbyterian. And the early feminist leader Elizabeth Cady Stanton was the daughter of a strict Presbyterian lawyer.

The denomination has also had some millionaires in its ranks, including George Westinghouse, William Dodge, and Sam Walton of Walmart fame. And some inventors were also part of the membership, including Cyrus McCormick, who invented the reaper that revolutionized American agriculture; Dr. James Naismith, who invented basketball; and William Flager, who some say invented Florida.

In the entertainment world, Jimmy Stewart was a member of the Beverly Hills Presbyterian Church, as is Kevin Costner. Dick Van Dyke was an active elder in the denomination and Mary Tyler Moore's character on her show was—what else?—a spunky Presbyterian. Will Rogers was a member, as was Roy Rogers. And Mister Rogers (who for more than 32 years has captivated children on public television) is an ordained Presbyterian minister.

The problem you'll have is that all of these people have operated at different times and in different venues. It will be difficult to work two or three famous names into a sentence at work without raising some eyebrows. But treat it as a challenge and give it a try. We can use the associations to promote our church!

BLESSED ARE THEY

If you are a manager or supervisor you should probably take any hiring recommendations from a Presbyterian pastor with a grain of salt. They are prone to give everyone a second chance.

PERCY T. PRESBY'S THOUGHTS ABOUT CELLULAR PHONES

Some Presbyterians believe that when God wanted us to talk to one another, He or She strung some wires.

WEEKENDS

On weekends, Presbyterian women are adept at

- ❑ doing the laundry.
- ❑ getting the groceries.
- ❑ making next week's meals.
- ❑ repairing clothing.
- ❑ cleaning the house.

On weekends, Presbyterian men are handy at

- ❑ changing light bulbs.
- ❑ making popcorn.
- ❑ explaining the infield fly rule.
- ❑ letting the phone ring.
- ❑ napping and hoping the neighbor will mow his lawn later in the day.

PERCY T. PRESBY'S LITTLE COMMENT ON LITERATURE AND LIQUOR ON WEEKENDS

Some Presbyterian men agree with Don McCraig, who said that the Scots make a good whiskey and in Bobby Burns they had a good poet, but he'd never drunk enough of the former to understand the latter.

THE WEEKEND PROJECTS

On occasion, the Presbyterian female half of the house is able to rouse her male counterpart to participate in a home improvement project. This usually occurs on Saturdays in the spring. Today many houses are bigger and older and harder to care for. And any project looks easy on one of those house-fixer TV shows. "Let's fix up the place" is the rallying cry.

Unfortunately, such endeavors require at least a modicum of skills. First, you have to chase down one of those orange-aproned persons at Home Depot to find whatever it is that you are looking for. The things you want are inevitably in other departments. You then persuade yourself to buy tools that you don't know how to use, for projects that even a licensed contractor shudders at.

After you take it all home you discover that neither of you is a Bob Vila. So the advice from here is to curb those do-it-yourself projects and wait for Sunday worship when the desire usually passes.

Unless, of course, you know what you are doing and are helping build Habitat for Humanity houses. Then that new deck you always wanted is probably a good idea.

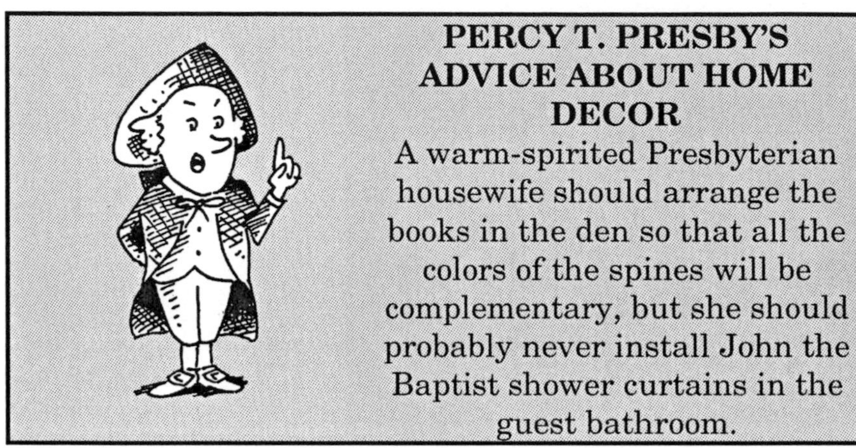

PERCY T. PRESBY'S ADVICE ABOUT HOME DECOR

A warm-spirited Presbyterian housewife should arrange the books in the den so that all the colors of the spines will be complementary, but she should probably never install John the Baptist shower curtains in the guest bathroom.

BLUE BLAZERS, LITTLE BLACK NOTHINGS, SHORTS, AND OVERALLS

What to wear? You may be confronted with this dilemma soon after you join our church. For the first month or so, you've worn your best bib and tucker every Sunday morning, relying on a sincere suit or modest dress to show your earnest worthiness.

But now it's social time and a chance to casually mingle and munch with your warm-hearted new comrades outside of the church parlors. If you live in a large eastern city, you should be alert when you are invited to someone's home. Punch with strawberries and even a splash of something alcoholic may be served. You should probably describe the punch, in typical Presbyterian understatement, as "awesome!"

As for dress, if you're a man, opt for the traditional blue blazer, gray slacks, and striped tie. There'll be so many of the fellows dressed that way at the affair that if all of you stand together you'll look like a boys' glee club.

If you're a woman, you can't go wrong if you choose your little black nothing, accompanied by the pearls you got as a high school graduation present from Aunt Lavinia that turned out to be fake. If you are older, the dress should have sleeves. Gloves add a nice touch.

That's the winter uniform. In the summer, it's white slacks for the men and a pastel cotton frock for the ladies. And for traditional eastern Presbyterian ladies, no black before (or white after) five.

What's the Frozen Chosen dress code in the South and the West and the Midwest? More informal, but not half as daring as Cher's three beads and a prayer.

Open-collar sports shirts are okay for the Presbyterian fella's in those places and sweaters and jeans for both guys and gals are welcomed in trend-setting California. Long shorts are even seen in sanctuaries there on Sunday. The shirts, blouses, slacks, and shorts don't even have to complement one another. And they can be of any color.

But that classic midwestern and southern uniform—bib overalls—hasn't quite made it for worship services or social events, even in the Presbyterian gatherings in rural areas where some 30 percent of our congregations are located. They do not seem to be seemly and therefore a sport shirt for the guys is recommended. Any color. A belt is sometimes okay. And for those female attendees in those areas, a simple little frock and low, sensible heels will do nicely.

You probably should remember all of this the next time you go out. But you should also take note of Henry David Thoreau's admonition to "beware of all enterprises that require new clothes."

FUNNY, HE DOESN'T LOOK PRESBYTERIAN

Presbyterian clergymen in everyday life are usually indistinguishable from other citizens. Although they often wear robes on Sundays and at funerals and at weddings inside the church, their civilian clothes normally conform to the norm in the outside world.

Oh, like their female colleagues, they will sometimes wear a clerical shirt and Roman collar on hospital visitations to avoid a lot of explaining to the nurses, but they usually opt for nondescript garb in most other civilian situations.

It is tempting, then—if you're a man—to imitate one of them just to see what will happen. You should probably resist this gambit for it often has unintended consequences.

One Atlanta fellow, bored with the prospect of yet another gathering where he knew no one, decided to pass himself off as a Presbyterian parson. He spent the evening listening to a remarkable number of tales of good deeds done, accompanied by solemn assurances that the world was not going to hell in a bushel basket. He also noted that everyone within a ten-foot radius cleaned up their language so much as to make eavesdropping decidedly uninteresting. All his fellow guests seemed hell bent on respectability.

So it's probably best to ignore the temptation to imitate a Presbyterian male pastor in your daily life. Unless you're seeking some sort of social quietness and have an ability to listen to people.

DIRTY WORDS

We Presbyterians are against sloth. We don't know quite what it is, but like pornography, we know it when we see it.

Some of us just like to say the word. *Sloth.* It sounds sort of furtive and naughty. Because practically nobody really knows what it means, it's easy to get a consensus against it because it just sounds so awful!

The same with the word *viscosity*. Just rolling it around in the mouth gives one a bit of a tingle! Viscosity.

Like name-dropping, it is admittedly difficult to work both of those words into a single sentence at a Presbyterian social function. But give it a shot. Your hostess will probably be impressed and it will get her mind off sex.

PERCY T. PRESBY'S FINDING ABOUT SEX

Many people have sex without guilt; many Presbyterians have guilt without sex.

MAKING WHOOPEE!

Presbyterians usually get upset with four-letter words. But as you have gathered by now from the talk in the church corridors, we have recently been truly flummoxed by a three-letter one—sex. It's a Presbyterian predicament, for it forces us to talk and read about what we don't want to talk and read about.

People say we are the folks who think condom is a slang term for condominium. And we seldom listen to that little "Alvin-the-Chipmunk-with-a-German-Accent," Dr. Ruth, because she's so—well—frank. As someone remarked about the English, how we Presbyterians reproduce is one of the wonders of the world. So it's no wonder that we got into a bit of a snit over a church report and some amendments to our church constitution that involved sexuality.

Although the issues have been around for years, the most recent contretemps started with a 200-page report back in 1991 titled "Keeping The Body and Soul Together." It was developed by a national task force and it recommended that the church relax its traditional objections against sexual relations between unmarried people and between homosexuals. As someone remarked, the report said that the denomination should turn the "Thou shalt nots" into "Thou shalts"—under certain conditions.

While we Presbyterians are reputedly among the more socially liberal of the Protestants, this document seemed to go a bit too far. For in spite of all the changes in society in the past few years, we have a tradition of being a rather strait-laced lot. Many of us were raised in a time when sex was dirty and the air was clean, instead of the other way around.

Then along came the sexual revolution. Easy access to the automobile and the pill gave everyone more freedom. And our gay and lesbian friends "came out."

Divorce is pretty common now and young people are starting their sex lives at an earlier age. And to maintain that the 29 percent of our membership who are single don't do some fooling around is probably naive. Changing lifestyles are bringing about changing mores.

The report was the result of a study by a nationally appointed task force of 17 ministers, laity, and health specialists. The document and its recommendations were submitted to the General Assembly at its meeting in Baltimore in the summer of 1991.

It tried to reconcile modern day practices of sexuality with the traditional biblical admonitions. While bowing to the supremacy of the Scriptures, it stated that "there is no single, consistent biblical ethic of sexuality." It recommended that the church not condemn "any sexual relations in which there is genuine equality and mutual respect." This would include relations between homosexual persons, adolescents, and unmarried heterosexuals. Celibacy should not be considered "the only moral option for single persons." The report also recommended that gay and lesbian candidates for the ministry be ordained immediately.

There was an immediate reaction. Half of the presbyteries rejected the report before the ink was really dry and a quarter of those demanded that it not even be considered by the General Assembly. The document never stood a chance in Baltimore. When it came to the floor of the G.A., it was set aside by a vote of 534 to 31.

The debate pitted the liberals against the conservatives of our moderate denomination, reminding everyone that when Presbyterians form a firing squad, they stand in a circle. The traditionalists cited the biblical injunctions against adultery and homosexuality. They seemed to believe that if anything goes, it will lead to everything going.

The liberals maintained that a Big-Tent Church must live in modern times and should be adaptable. They stressed tolerance for all in our denomination. Besides, they pointed out, we now have a lot of alumni. Why not be more inclusive?

The traditionalists carried the day. But as the issue has continued to simmer in the individual churches, some other views have begun to emerge. Some moderate Presbyterians have studied the 1991 document in a calmer light and have found its language to be very vague.

It is full of phrases such as "eroticized equality" and "right relatedness" and "holistic understanding." Some believe that such ambiguous language obscures rather than elucidates, and that the writers, like those that Talleyrand condemned, used words to conceal rather than reveal. To others, this was useful, for like Humpty Dumpty, they think that words should mean what they want them to mean.

And then in 1996, we Presbyterians again took up the issue of sex. Amendment B, the so-called fidelity and chastity amendment, was proposed to become a part of the constitution of the church. This overture to the General Assembly was designed to change the *Book of Order* in order to support fidelity in all relationships. To some, it was a reaction to the 1991 so-called "Love Is All You Need" report.

To others, it was a strengthening of the ban on ordaining "self-affirming, practicing homosexuals" previously passed by the G.A. back in 1978. (That ban was countered by the bold declaration of the flamboyant writer, Quentin Crisp, who when once asked if he was a practicing homosexual said that no, he didn't practice because he was already perfect.)

Amendment B in 1996 included a provision that the only acceptable sexual expression for ordained people (ministers, elders, deacons) is between a man and a woman within the context of marriage, or "chastity in singleness." The amendment was introduced to and passed by the General Assembly and went to the presbyteries later that year, where it was approved by a very narrow 50.6 percent of the vote. It went into effect in June 1997.

It caused dismay and dissension within and among our 11,216 churches, and caused one member to drop a proposed book she was planning to title *The Joy of Presbyterian Sex*. The publisher reportedly said it would be too thin a volume.

But in a stunning move at the General Assembly in Syracuse, New York in the same year that Amendment B took effect, the commissioners approved a proposed new amendment, the so-called "Fidelity and Integrity Amendment"—Amendment A—that opened the door and effected a compromise intended to temper the rule.

That substitute amendment went back to the presbyteries where it was defeated. So Amendment B remains in effect today. And as of this writing, there is supposedly a moratorium (or sabbatical) on the discussion of this issue at the G.A. while further studies are undertaken.

But in July of 2000, the G.A. approved an amendment forbidding ministers from conducting same-sex unions. If ratified by the presbyteries, it will go into effect in 2001.

Some members say that God really doesn't care about who's doing what and to whom. Others maintain that because any amendments apply only to officers of the church (pastors, elders, deacons), it won't ever affect them. Still others liken it all to Saint Augustine's philosophy when he asked God for chastity and continence, but "not just now."

Some members believe that there is a biblical ban on homosexual activity. They say that the denomination should stand firm in its defense of a strict morality.

Most of us agree with noted Presbyterian authors Kirkpatrick and Hoper, who advise that we should "be sensitive to and care for each other," for a Reformed Church is always reforming, and "warm hearts and pastoral spirits are needed as never before in the Presbyterian Church (U.S.A.)."

Although Calvin is probably turning over in his grave, the dialogue about sex is just one more bit of evidence that you have joined a vital and energized 21st-century church that is addressing some of the most perplexing questions in a forthright manner. As the Cole Porter song had it, "Birds do it, bees do it..." It appears that we Presbyterians have now publicly admitted that we do it, too.

PERCY T. PRESBY'S QUIP ABOUT ENTERTAINMENT

Some Presbyterians think that *Naughty Marietta* was an adult film, and they are still a little concerned about what made *The Merry Widow* merry.

RELIGIOUS BUMPER STICKERS

MORMON (Salt Lake City)
When the Church Speaks, All Thinking Has Been Done

METHODIST (Minneapolis)
*Luke 13:30**

HOLY POWER CHURCH (Biloxi)
If you think I'm Jesus, honk

---

*"The last shall be first," a reference to the area's 1991 World Champion baseball team.

BAPTIST (Little Rock)
If You Love Jesus—TITHE! Anyone Can Honk

PRESBYTERIAN (Boston)
Presbyterians Do It Decently and in Order

PRESBYTERIAN PROPINQUITY

Whatever your views about sex, everyone seems to agree that you eventually have to get near somebody to engage in it. And to get closer to people you may be persuaded to attend a church retreat sometime during your experience in the denomination. Although there won't be any dilly-dallying, there will be a promise of some Presbyterian intimacy.

You may be asked to sign up for a weekend at a church camp in the woods near a lake. The purpose of it will be to allow some friendly members of the congregation to get away from the madding crowd to refresh their souls. They will tell you that you can walk, swim, meditate, and commune with nature with a bunch of other wonderful folks from your church.

The idea is that in that group you will find warm kinship and sweet fellowship, while being embraced by a fond and endearing church family. The notion seems to be that close proximity will bring about love, understanding, and affection. Anybody who really believes that, however, has clearly never ridden the subway in New York City during the rush hour.

You'll probably eat some food that is often quite bland and sleep on lumpy mattresses in bunk beds in leaky cabins. Everything will smell a bit musty.

It will rain, of course—all day—on both days of the affair. This will force everyone to spend even more time together inside the main lodge, playing ping-pong and board games and discussing life. You will become close to some nurturing and amiable folk who have the very best of intentions and who provide a caring discipleship. Their constant presence and compassion may eventually get to you, however, so that at some time during the weekend you'll decide that you agree with the old saying that one could love humanity all right, if the darn people wouldn't keep getting in the way.

A surprise, however, usually awaits you when you return to the outside world. During the next week you'll find yourself more mellow and—dare you admit it?—more tolerant of the gentle foibles and follies of other folk and most important—of yourself. And for a long time afterward you'll find yourself exchanging knowing, warm glances with those wonderful brothers and sisters in Christ who shared the weekend with you. It was—you'll then have to admit—a marvelous experience! Give it a try!

PRESBYTERIANS USUALLY DON'T TRUST

- ❑ freeway gas station mechanics.
- ❑ salesmen who knock at their door.
- ❑ women who chew gum.
- ❑ TV weatherpersons.
- ❑ anyone called "Honest John."

PERCY T. PRESBY'S PRESCRIPTION FOR PARENTING

Presbyterian mothers should tell their kids to watch repeats of *The Andy Griffith Show*, because look at how well Opie turned out.

THE KINGDOM OF HEAVEN!

Little kids in ancient times ran merrily with the wind in their faces and skipped and jumped gleefully into rain puddles! In rural America there was nothing so wonderful as a somersault in a haymow. And as one grew, there were hide-and-go-seek games and cannonballs off the dock, all of which contributed to the sweet, sweet spirit of childhood. But some say that it took some Presbyterian kids to devise one of the most exhilarating pleasures of early youth.

It's swinging by the hands between two loving adults during a walk. It helps if that walk is on what many say are the three greatest words in the English language: "a summer afternoon."

Percy T. Presby maintains that this little exercise originated with some youngsters and their folks in the late 1500s in Scotland during the time of John Knox. It was a Kodak moment before there was a Kodak. Today, it is enjoyed by parents and grandparents and children in many other denominations throughout the world.

But Percy T. says it was begun by some Calvinists who viewed this glorious activity as another wondrous example of the natural joy of God's children—"for such is the kingdom of heaven!" It's pleasure at its best!

If you are a parent or grandparent it will remind you of the marvelous new experiences you discovered when you were a kid and the innocent trust you had that you would never be dropped. Nostalgic murmurings will kick in as you remember how glorious it felt to be a child! As Buddha once noted, "If you wish to know the Divine, feel the wind on your face and the warm sun on your hand."

If you somehow haven't remembered or discovered this delightful activity yet, get your spouse or another adult and give it a try. Even if you have to borrow a little kid. Whee!

DANCING ALL NIGHT

If you are a parent of a Presbyterian adolescent, you're going to have to deal with what Ecclesiastes calls "a time to dance." It's probably common knowledge among your kids that you've forgotten how to move your feet to music in any coordinated fashion—if indeed you ever knew how. But now your apparent Christian parental role is to somehow try to control the avalanche of debauchery among the young on the dance floor. You should approach this assignment with a sigh, and with a bit of history in mind.

Even before the birth of Christ, Cicero observed that "no sane man will dance." It didn't stop anybody. And when David danced joyously in the nude in a paean to God, everyone thought he was mad, but at least he did it alone. Eventually there were some man-dancing-with-man situations, and finally women got to join in. In the 17th century, Calvinists only reluctantly accepted the quadrille, where men and women bowed and touched hands ever so briefly in various prescribed configurations on the dance floor.

They saved their real ire for the waltz, that wicked romp to sinfully gay music in three-quarter time. When it was imported from Germany to Scotland in the early 18th century, it was said to have threatened the very fabric of Presbyterian society. Dancers twirled at a dizzying pace, which intoxicated the mind and reportedly led to some inevitable consequences off the ballroom floor.

Face to face, the dancers whirled in abandon to the oom-pah-pah of "The Blue Danube," with the man's gloved hand actually touching the lady's waist, and his partner's gloved hand resting right there on his shoulder. Their growing passion could often be detected by observing their flaring nostrils, and they say that some Presbyterian fathers kept buckets of water at the ready to throw on those couples who got carried away by it all. By 1892, things had degenerated to the point that a best-selling book titled *From the Ballroom to Hell* pretty much summed up the situation.

Things got worse, however, what with the introduction of the two-step at the turn of the century, and the ragtime music that set toes to tapping even more. The fox trot and the jazz-influenced cakewalk gave way to the hot-blooded tango, which added an exotic foreign influence to the gyrations on the dance floor. In the 1920s, Presbyterian mothers reportedly took to their beds when their daughters did the Charleston. The dance was widely viewed as immoral, and fruitlessly condemned from coast to coast in Presbyterian pulpits.

By the time the 1930s rolled around, bringing with them the Latin licentiousness of the rumba (where all the movement was from the hips down), many Presbyterians were said to be ready to call for God to come get them. But then along came the athletic Lindy (or the jitterbug) of the 1940s with its frenzied movements, fueled by teenage vigor. At least the dance wasn't provocative (or so it was thought) because it evidently took so much energy on the dance floor that there was little left for off-the-floor shenanigans!

Parents were further encouraged with the introduction of the do-your-own-thing dance era, with the twist and the monkey and the frug, where the partners never touched. The persuasive beat-beat-beat of disco in the 1970s made them groan again, but at least the touching was usually fleeting.

But then came the 1990s and the bump-and-grind of the Lambada. To most Presbyterians, it was simply the most terrible dance ever devised. Its motions convinced many that that's all she wrote, folks. God is about to wrap things up. But it also died out.

And was replaced by country line dancing with its push-tush, as well as the internationally popular Macarena. Although the song tells the story of a vain girl who wants to cheat on her boyfriend, the pulsing beat inspires movements that are so bland that a vice president of the United States once threatened to dance it at the Democratic convention. Today some Presbyterian Sunday School teachers use the Macarena movements to teach their little ones "Jesus Loves Me."

Now as a parent, you're maybe faced with the proposition that you should be of some influence to your high-spirited adolescents on the dance floor as they try out some new fad. Sorry, but it's a hopeless task that should not even be undertaken. Oh, you might try suggesting the waltz, that once-wicked innovation that nearly brought down civilization, or the innocent hokey-poky—which maintains that it is what it's all about. But frankly, you probably haven't got a chance of influencing anything in the dance arena. About the only thing you can do is to inform your kids that Presbyterians usually don't polka.

PERCY T. PRESBY'S MAXIM ABOUT KIDS AND MUSIC

Some Presbyterian parents think that a jazz band is the Boston Pops.

LEAVING HOME

Presbyterian daughters go off to college to major in boys and their brothers go to learn how to drink beer. They both elevate pizza to the highest level of cuisine.

Like most kids newly on their own, they occasionally rebel. Their form of bouncing their heads on the ceiling of parental authority, however, often differs from other young people.

Some Presbyterian college freshmen have to learn that (1) running with a lollipop in their mouth, (2) not putting toilet paper on the seat in a public restroom, and (3) going swimming after dinner before an hour is up, are not considered rebellions by their new classmates. So the denomination's college kids sometimes rent a video movie and don't rewind it. Their ultimate act of defiance, reportedly, is to deliberately wear dirty underwear with holes in it while on a car trip home as a sort of silent protest over what their mother always taught them. They half hope for an accident.

Let it all happen joyfully and try not to smile. For they have the keys to the Kingdom and are a part of God's perfect plan!

PERCY T. PRESBY'S WARNING ABOUT CHILD RAISING

A few Presbyterian young adults sue their parents for not abusing them as a child, for otherwise they now have no good reason for being so temporarily unhappy.

PATIENCE, PATIENCE

In addition to attempting to regulate our children's and our own lives, we Presbyterians have to deal daily with the fascinating outside world. And there are a great number of quirky things and lively people out there that can sometimes aggravate even the most loving, mild-mannered members of our church. Not all us can be members of the Forbearance Presbyterian Church, the delightful, but fictional, church of columnist Charlotte Johnstone in *Horizons* magazine.

So we must occasionally inure ourselves to the gripes and moans and acts of some other wonderful folks who have seemingly been placed here on earth specifically to test our annoyance level. Arrrgh!

Instead, we should tolerate, cherish, and embrace them, for they all have God's goodness in their hearts. We should look at all the wonderful things that happen in our daily life in a loving and optimistic Presbyterian manner with a great generosity of spirit and love for all mankind. For as that great sage Dolly Parton says, "If ya' want the rainbow, ya' gotta' put up with the rain!"

PERCY T. PRESBY'S VERITY ABOUT PEOPLE

Presbyterians believe that all those letters to Ann Landers are made up, because there just can't be that many people who are "Outraged in North Dakota."

A PRESBYTERIAN'S IDEAS OF HELL HERE ON EARTH

- ❑ Listening to a 30-minute drum solo
- ❑ Watching people drink Scotch and 7-Up
- ❑ Not having possession of the TV remote control
- ❑ Running over an already squished cat on the road
- ❑ People behind you talking continuously during the movie

PERCY T. PRESBY'S OBSERVATION ABOUT POLITICIANS

Many modern-day Presbyterians will vote for anybody who promises to make the use of a cellular phone in a restaurant a felony, and telephone solicitation at any time punishable by the death penalty.

THE SECOND TEN

Sometime during the 1970s, a Methodist and discriminating nut by the name of Warren E. Reed handed down some advice for dealing with people and the *sturm und drang* of daily life. He sought to counsel himself by helping to control his occasional irritation and impatience with his wonderful fellow human beings. The result was a document he conceived as he contemplated his mortality for three hours from the top of a stuck Ferris wheel at the amusement park near his home in Excelsior, Minnesota.

After this epiphany, the parchment found its way into the hands of his brother and some other Presbyterians who promptly appropriated it as their own. Many of them feel that today our country is one of divorce, downsizing, disillusion, and in-your-face confrontation at a high decibel level. There is a desperate need for sweet fellowship between and among our comrades and companions on this planet.

So they advise you to study the document and apply its admonitions in your struggle to maintain some equilibrium in your daily relationships with those fascinating, different others in our denomination. And in your association with yourself and good people everywhere who seek a sunnier day. In these days of road rage, runway rage, school rage, and religious rage, this little list might be useful in helping to prayerfully counsel the human heart and allow us all to "live in peace with one another" (Thessalonians).

…and there shalt be a second ten commandments that thou shalt give unto thyself, and these shalt be:

- ❑ Thou shalt forever be easy to get along with, even when things are NOT done thy way.
- ❑ Thou shalt at times use discretion and keep thy big mouth shut—but thou shalt not remain silent at ALL times, for it is well that thou shouldst occasionally let it be known what is in thy heart and in thy mind about this, that, and the other.

- ❑ Thou shalt endeavor to keep thyself flexible and seek thy enjoyment in pleasing not only thyself, but others as well, by doing it their way ONCE in a while.
- ❑ Thou shalt be expected to express thy pleasure as well as to share thy problems, for thou shalt find that in so doing, thy pleasures shalt be multiplied, and thy problems shalt be divided.
- ❑ Thou shalt remember always, however, that what thou ART speaks so loud that often one cannot hear what is SAID by thee—and thy actions art therefore more important than thy words.
- ❑ Thou shalt remember that those that surround thee, like thyself, art busy struggling with themselves as well as with the rest of the world, and that thy job shalt be to help them win this battle by finding time for words of encouragement as well as criticism.
- ❑ Thou shalt refrain from placing undue emphasis upon the material things of this life and the darn price tag that goeth with each.
- ❑ Thou shalt remember, however, that certain obligations must always be met, that these shalt always be greater than thy resources, and it shalt be necessary for thee to picketh and to chooseth—and to be flexible in such matters.
- ❑ Thou shalt remember that it is thy duty—and it shouldst be thy pleasure—to serve all those who surround thee, for in so doing, thou shalt then have every right to expect them to serve thee.
- ❑ Finally, thou shalt remember that other people as well as thee shalt have faults, and that whilst many of these canst be corrected, there shalt be others which can only be accepted—and it shalt be a rule that the faults of both thee and them shalt be accepted with a big cotton-pickin,' chicken-pluckin' smile upon thy face!

PERCY T. PRESBY'S DISCOVERY ABOUT OUR MEMBERS

A recent informal survey of some Presbyterians revealed that only 5 percent thought they would end up in hell, but 38 percent knew someone who was going there.

A COMPLIMENT A DAY

Some folks set aside one day each year to practice Random Acts of Kindness. Some Reform Jews celebrate an annual Mitzvah Day—a time of good deeds. Many Presbyterians become even more tolerant of their fellow persons by praising someone—EVERY day. They say it does wonders for both the giver and receiver.

A compliment engenders a positive feeling to those who bestow it ("Great job!") and a little smile to those who receive it ("Thank you!"). And it doesn't cost anything.

Looking for the virtues in others ennobles us. And by accepting a compliment, the recipient brightens with the praise. It's a feel-good exchange that puts a spring into the step of both parties.

Complimenting someone is an antidote for negativism and a sure cure for incivility. As Mark Twain once noted, "I can live a whole month on a compliment." Try one with somebody, today!

THE PRESBYTERIAN BLUSH

When you compliment a fellow member of the church, however, the response you get may reveal a common Presbyterian malady—embarrassment. We church members don't take praise very well and blush quite easily. We tend to look away or down at our shoes or wince and try to overlook the favorable remark. Or we deflect the compliment in some way.

This also creates an uneasiness in any onlookers. As the writer Ian Frazier notes, "Those who are embarrassed avert their eyes, and those who see the embarrassed ones do the same, embarrassed on their behalf." It's all so Presbyterian.

Some of our members, however, seem unusually adept at handling compliments. A few actually seem to seek them out. It all makes for a wonderful variety of fascinating folk in the church of the Frozen Chosen. And a diversity that is at once unsettling and inspiring!

BLESS US ALL!

As Reverend Max Lucardo has noted, "Though different, we are the same." We should take to heart the admonition in Romans 14:1, which says that one should "welcome with open arms fellow believers who don't see things the way you do." And we should embrace all those who think and act and behave in other ways.

For we should join together in joyful gratitude and Christian caring, by loving whom God loves—everyone. And we should celebrate our glorious diversity. For as the pastor whom I hear preach regularly in Northport, New York reminds us, "the presence of a Christian community does not mean the absence of differences."

Chapter Seven

THE PRESBYTERIAN PSYCHE

PERCY T. PRESBY'S THOUGHTS ABOUT OUR PSYCHE

Presbyterian psychology usually leads one to live a life of quiet discourse; the people who violate their own privacy on the *Jerry Springer Show* are not Presbyterians.

EMOTIONS

Always remember that good, old-fashioned Presbyterians do not often let their feelings run away from them. They usually do not understand lonely people who cheer when the mailman comes, or those who sob uncontrollably when they hear "Jingle Bells" at Christmastime.

Long time members say that your countenance should reflect a restrained but loving compassion for your fellow human beings, and that you should try to keep a stiff upper lip even in the most trying of circumstances.

Leave the weeping and breast-beating and shouting to our Fundamentalist friends. Folks say that they will thank you for it.

PERCY T. PRESBY'S THOUGHTS ABOUT FURROWED BROWS

When Presbyterians aren't worrying, they are worried about what they are not worrying about.

DEMEANOR

Many folks say that the Presbyterian mindset also reveres politeness. This does not allow the male to use his sharp elbows while moving through the crowd at a summer softball game. Inching forward with an apologetically murmured "'Scuse me" is the ticket. And the older male Presbyterian still opens doors for the ladies and walks on the outside of the street when accompanying them on errands.

It's said that they, in turn, often register their displeasure at someone who has made a botch of things by a discreet little cluck. If it happens twice, they reportedly respond by knitting faster.

Everything in the psychology of the older members of our denomination favors the delicious seemliness of life. Someday you'll find it wonderful!

PERCY T. PRESBY'S RECOMMENDED CARD FOR THE WALLET

"I am a Presbyterian. In case of an accident, don't call anybody. I was born to suffer."

TOGETHERNESS

Many people in our denomination reject a private Christianity, avowing that we should share our belief with others in a "connective manner." According to church writings, Presbyterians belong to what is called "a fraternity of believers," which is a "voluntary camaraderie of *confessional intimacy* (emphasis added)." We do have a close-knit church family, but this can be taken too far. You probably shouldn't ask one of us how much money we make.

PRESBYTERIANS USUALLY FEEL GUILTY WHEN

- ❑ they mistakenly give someone the wrong travel directions.
- ❑ they don't find time to visit a friend in the hospital.
- ❑ they receive a book as a gift and don't finish it.
- ❑ they take the last two deviled eggs at the potluck supper.
- ❑ they break off too big a hunk of bread during communion—and enjoy it!

THE PRESBYTERIAN CURSE

Many of our members often feel a certain proprietorship about guilt. We know we didn't invent it, however, and resent the Jews for getting there first. And then we feel guilty about our resentment.

So we quietly try to make up for it all by being nice, and helping everybody. Hurrah!

THE MISSIONARIES ARE COMING! THE MISSIONARIES ARE COMING!

According to the *Book of Order*, one of the missions of our church is missionary. So there are many Presbyterians who support worthy causes in far-off lands (the so-called Salt-Water Efforts) as well as here at home. The missionaries spread the Good News!

But there are others who campaign—and compete—for funds after services every Sunday in the hallways outside the sanctuary in many Presbyterian churches across the land. One has to run a sort of card-table-gauntlet to get to the coffee hour.

For there are wonderful folk there soliciting funds to eliminate halitosis in old dogs, and those helpful souls who are seeking a donation to reform the people who worship the Shroud of Elvis. It's said to have been credited with 93 miracles including dramatic weight gain.

There are often some compassionate people who think everything they see on television is real, and for the last 20 years have been trying to raise money to get those folks off *Gilligan's Island.* You may even run into that delightful little lady who travels in a van from church to church seeking funds to convert the citizens of a village in the south of France who pray to a 75-foot statue of Jerry Lewis. She says that when you push a button, Jerry sings two choruses of "You'll Never Walk Alone."

Our guilt tells us that we should give to all such causes generously, and give we do. We wouldn't be Presbyterians otherwise. So relax. There's no use fighting it. Pry open your pocketbook. And smile. God loves a cheerful giver!

PERCY T. PRESBY'S DEFINITION OF A PRESBYTERIAN #3

A Presbyterian is one who prefers to view injustice as simply good intentions gone awry.

PSYCHING OUT THE RIGHT ONE

If your minister moves on to another position, you may become involved in helping secure a replacement. This process will test the Presbyterian psyche and may try your patience.

First, an Interim Pastor Nominating Committee will be formed. This sort-of-second-team group will seek somebody who will take on the full-time job on a temporary basis for a year or so. While this search goes on, the pulpit will be filled with visiting preachers from one Sunday to the next.

Meanwhile, the first team—the Pastor Nominating Committee (PNC)—for a permanent pastor—will be starting to discharge its responsibilities. If you become a member of this body, you will participate in the writing of a new Church Profile. This is a sort of a group analysis, without a couch. The resulting document will be the culmination of countless meetings that will thoroughly reexamine your local church and restate its Christian mission and goals.

Then, after a new job description is written and published, dossiers will be received from interested candidates. Those that survive the first cut will be interviewed and the committee will listen to the final three or four candidates preach at a neutral site on a series of Sunday mornings. Your group will then recommend one of them to your membership, the candidate will come and preach to all of you some Sabbath morning, and a vote will be taken to call that person to become your pastor.

The entire process typically takes about two years and is spelled out in some detail for the local nominating committees by the presbytery.

What they don't tell you, however, is how to deal with candidates that have a sense of humor. This is because some Presbyterian churches reportedly do not officially recognize the existence of this uplifting psychological condition. And they therefore have evidently developed no policy about it.

Our denomination has never really been known as a joyous one. We sometimes seem to operate in a humor-free zone. It's been said that Calvin put a man in jail for three days for laughing in church and some reports have it that he sometimes woke up in the middle of the night, worrying that somewhere in the world, someone was having a good time.

So a member should supposedly be ever on guard against true levity, for they say a laugh could be fatal. Some outside observers maintain that for a Presbyterian to be really happy, there should probably be a sort of aura of cloudiness surrounding things. A few physicians—of other faiths, of course—say that many of us suffer from a wonderfully named condition known as *anhedonia*—the incapacity for experiencing happiness.

The tone is often inevitably set by the local minister. So all candidates for that job should probably be psychologically examined for any evidence that there is any funny or lighthearted stuff in their background. To ignore this detail is said to court disaster. It may even bring on a calamity such as the one that reportedly occurred in a church in Kansas City, Missouri in the 1960s.

There, the PNC recommended and the congregation called a young man who had impeccable credentials and a demeanor of sanctimonious piety. They failed to discover, though, that even on days as bad as a rained-out ball game, he had been seen to laugh a bit.

For the first month or so, things went swimmingly. But then the new guy began to lose it. He had a sense of humor—and a rather bizarre one, at that.

It became evident with his reading of the Scriptures at the Sunday morning services. Normally, he read ponderously, but with great feeling. But on one sunny morning, for unknown reasons, he began to gradually dissolve into uncontrollable laughter as he read through that day's text.

It started with a slight upturn on the right side of his mouth, which he covered with his hand. Between long pauses and deep breaths, a series of s-s-s-s's escaped from his pursed lips, as he fought to control himself. With his hand over his mouth, his speech became somewhat unintelligible and this seemed to exacerbate things. A giggle or two escaped, and tears began to well up in his eyes.

A laugh was building and working its way to the surface, and in an effort to suppress it, he hunched over and his shoulders began to shake. But it was to no avail, as he finally erupted in a barked "Har! Har! Har!" just as he finished the reading and sat down.

The congregation was stunned. They looked at one another. It was all decidedly un-Presbyterian!

The minister apologized to the chairman of the Worship Committee at the coffee hour, and people sort of shrugged off the incident. But it began to happen with more frequency on some subsequent Sundays.

It usually started somewhere near the beginning of his reading of the Scriptures. A grin would bring on a giggle and the giggle would bring on a chuckle. In an effort to restore some solemnity, the minister would lower his voice an octave and adopt a super-serious mien. His hand would go to his face and he would bite his lips or his tongue or put a knuckle in his mouth in an attempt to stifle the forthcoming laugh.

In a frantic tactic to get through the reading before he lost control, he would pick up the pace, making the partially smothered words even more incomprehensible. On some occasions, he made it to the end before he collapsed back into his chair beside the pulpit, with great whoops of delight! But some Sundays, after a gallant battle, he would surrender to his own merriment midway through the scripture reading, and it would have to be abandoned.

He finally confessed to the session that his breakups were triggered by certain words in the Bible. *Shalt* was one, and *verily* was another. He had never had this problem before, he said, but "didn't *verily* sound kinda' funny?"

The session asked him to make a list of all the words that set him off, and when the Scripture lesson for that Sunday contained any of them, they assigned someone to read the passages for him. They also insisted that he get some counseling.

But the reader thing didn't work out because most of the folk who had the ability to stand up there and read in public had also become afflicted with the malady. There is nothing more tempting than the possibility of laughter in a forbidden setting. Once an idea is psychologically planted in the mind, it is dangerous.

By now, of course, the entire congregation was also aware of the problem words, and those who were following along with the reading in the pew Bibles could see when such a word was coming up. And they would snicker and chuckle in anticipation.

It was contagious! Their reactions fed the readers and the readers fed the reactions, and when one of them came to one of the words, a glance over at the minister would be enough to set them all off, filling the sanctuary with restrained chuckles.

The minister reported no progress from the psychiatric sessions he was attending, so finally the clerk of the session—the aptly named Clarence C. Toomley—decided that enough was enough. He was an assistant in a funeral parlor and a sort of dull and pious man. No one had ever seen him listen to a joke, let alone tell one. He would put a stop to all this nonsense once and for all, he said, and break the humor chain by reading from the Scriptures himself the next time one of those words was in one of the passages.

And he almost pulled it off. As he rose and approached the pulpit on that Sabbath, there was a nearly palpable tension in the room. The congregation was deadly silent and especially attentive. Here was their stern savior come to do battle and smite the hilarity devil!

As Toomley began the reading, there was a titter in the back, but he silenced that person with a scowl. As he continued, he seemed to gather strength. His voice became stronger and more self-assured. He was on a roll!

But as he approached one of the dangerous words, the old fella' began to falter. Three passages before it, he began to slow down and take deep breaths. A glimmer of a smile was seen to cross his face, and his voice became strangulated. Was he actually stifling a laugh?

From the right side of the sanctuary came a little giggle and then another from the front, near the choir. The minister in his chair beside the pulpit was having a hard time keeping a straight face. Some titters floated up to the pulpit as the clerk got closer to the word, and it became apparent that he was really struggling to control himself.

Two passages before it, Toomley gave way to a little snort himself, and that brought a further response from the congregation. A communal wave of glee was building. He fought it and his own emotions. He cleared his throat. He looked to the ceiling. He gripped the sides of the pulpit tightly.

But when he finally reached the passage with the word in it, he paused, dropped his head, and emitted a little resigned sigh. The absurdity of it all had finally gotten to him. As he read on, a sort of beatific grin spread over his face. He was giving up. The struggle was over. He could contain himself no longer!

From somewhere in his nether regions, a rumbling roar started, and when he got to the word *verily*, it erupted into a bellowing guffaw that engulfed him and rolled out over the congregation! They responded with a cacophony of laughter that threatened to bring down the walls!

Gone. They were all gone. Some folks bent over the pews with tears streaming down their cheeks, while others clung to one another in abandonment! A few staggered to their feet, their faces contorted with hilarious hysteria as they tried to make it to the exits!

At the pulpit, Toomley was helpless himself as he alternately bent over and pounded the railings with his fist, or leaned back in joyous roaring surrender to the demons that possessed him. Holding his sides, he finally fell to the floor, unable to stand upright in the face of the laughter that consumed them all!

The congregation's howling continued for ten minutes, and after a few moments of sporadic giggling, started up again for another five minutes. The choir director finally took charge and canceled the rest of the service.

The minister left the next week, and eventually found an administrative post at a synod where he didn't have to publicly read from the Bible. A series of visiting preachers finally broke the humor chain at the local church. And after an interim pastor, the Pastor Nominating Committee recommended (and the church finally hired) an elderly minister who claimed that he hadn't laughed since 1954. Even though he sometimes couldn't remember to shave both sides of his face, he got along fine with everybody and never even cracked a smile, until his retirement five years later.

So if you get on a PNC, some folks say that you should probably remember to quiz each candidate very thoroughly about all of this. They recommend that you urge those applying for the call to take some tests to confirm they are at least somewhat humorless. It may save everybody a whole lot of trouble and establish what some outside folks appear to believe is the traditional psychological image of our church. For they say that we Presbys are often a few french fries short of a Happy Meal.

On the other hand, there is a growing tendency to include "a sense of humor" as one of the attributes desired in a new pastor in the Ministry Opportunities advertisements in *Monday Morning*, the magazine for church leaders, and in the lay magazine, *Presbyterians Today*. They seem to agree with St. Augustine's notion that God requires us to be happy.

So you just might find it refreshing to help select a good-natured shepherd who relishes the many funny delights and richness in life and who will help foster a festive fellowship of believers. Perhaps he or she can give your members an occasional little chuckle that will gladden the depths of everyone's heart and help bring an ineffable joy to God's people here on earth.

Your call. Either way, bless us all!

PERCY T. PRESBY'S DEFINITION OF HAPPINESS

For some Presbyterians, it is the infrequent but wonderful sensation that happens when one defeats a fellow committee member in a showdown vote.

GUILTY AS CHARGED

For other Presbyterians, happiness consists of participating in what Percy T. Presby says are the three greatest words in the English language, "Sunday afternoon nap." For still other Presbyterians, there is another form of happiness. We view a yummy elixir as one of life's most delicious and deepest pleasures. We're chocoholics.

We will take the stuff wherever we can get it—a chocolate malt on a hot day and some hot cocoa on a cold day and a hot fudge sundae on any day. Then there are cookies and cream and chocolate kisses and Butterfingers and Snickers that are all reminders that life is GOOD! And fudge, that nirvana on a plate, and a Whitman Sampler. They are all God's reward for being one of the disciples of Jesus!

We've been known to go to a great many lengths to coddle our psychological addiction. We have sometimes swiped some of the miniature bars from the kid's Halloween bags and sampled the chocolate bunnies from their Easter baskets. We are quite shameless, for we'll even occasionally have M & Ms with our breakfast food. And a double chocolate cake for desert at a potluck dinner is heaven!

Most of us are satisfied that we only gained 22 pounds last year and lost 20, and in spite of the fact that "a moment on the lips is ten years on the hips," a visit to that capital of chocolate in Hershey, Pennsylvania is about the closest to heaven that we can get without actually going there. The air even smells like our psychological condition. Even so, too much of a good thing sometimes makes one wonder if they have really given broccoli a fair chance. But as Mae West is supposed to have remarked, "too much of a good thing is wonderful!"

If you are one of us, you probably should curb your instinct for Presbyterian happiness and not get up right now and go seek a chocolate fix in the kitchen. On the other hand, a bit of that sinful essence of life might make the remainder of the reading of this little book more enjoyable. Just a thought.

PERCY T. PRESBY'S TAKE ON GUSTATORY DELIGHTS

Presbyterians are constitutionally unable to suck on a Lifesaver for more than five seconds without biting into it.

A SPIRITUAL REMINDER

About an hour north of San Francisco, in the middle of the countryside, sits a half-timbered English inn, complete with a cozy, low-ceilinged tavern. It appeals mightily to Scottish and British expatriates, Anglophiles, and wayfaring strangers, who revel in the charming premises. It's been there for some time.

In the beamed tap room, over the large walk-in fireplace, is a wonderful aphorism. Carved in big letters on the enormous timber that serves as a mantel is this adage:

Death Knocked At The Door:
Faith Answered And No One Was There

Nobody is quite sure of the origin of the saying or how it got there. But speculation centers around a Presbyterian who had something to do with the construction of the establishment.

It seems a bit out of place in the pub-like drinking hall. But then, it's probably most appropriate, for we Presbyterians can psychologically use all the spiritual reminders we can get, from wherever and whoever the source.

OUR FRIENDS

There is a wonderful spirit of ecumenism today among the various Christian denominations as well as between Christians and Jews and those of other faith traditions. And we draw inspiration from one another, understanding that we are all God's children though we may differ in some minor ways. Most of us agree with the sentiment *Spero pacen religionum* (I hope for peace among religions).

People of other denominations, however, have created certain pictures of the Presbyterians over the years. And we, in turn, have developed particular images of our friends in other faiths. Many of the lighthearted descriptions have, in fact, been originated by our comrades themselves. Fortunately, there are really very few differences between us all, but according to Percy T. Presby and the jokesters in other religious traditions:

- ❑ Methodists love fiery sermons, change ministers as often as they change clothes, and some think that *The Power of Positive*

Thinking by Dr. Norman Vincent Peale (who was once a Methodist) has something to do with it.

- ❑ Lutherans are blond, tack things up on bulletin boards a lot, and like music of all sorts, as long as it's by Bach.
- ❑ Episcopalians are Catholics Lite, who have one-third less guilt, and call themselves "Whiskeypalians" because they say that when four of them get together there's always a fifth.
- ❑ United Church of Christers have venerated democracy to a high art but are really closet Presbyterians, because they admit that they secretly would like at least some national authority in their lives.
- ❑ Jews joke that they are the only people who have mothers; they invented humor and Chinese food and some say that attending a Woody Allen movie is a religious observance.
- ❑ Baptists say "Amen" a lot, clap along to gospel music, tote Bibles to monster truck rallies, throw people in the river, and sometimes call themselves The Catholic Church of the Confederate States.
- ❑ Fundamentalists somehow manage to get born twice, and go on television a lot to beg for money to help pay for the experience.
- ❑ Mormons own Utah outright and they have one big choir; each man has three wives and they say that they are a religion that became a people.
- ❑ Unitarians come from other faiths, are smart, and are so liberal that they don't even have to go to church; in the South, people burn question marks on their lawns.
- ❑ And how do Presbyterians view themselves? Because some 18 percent of us were once followers of John Wesley, many think that we are simply Methodists with pretensions.

PERCY T. PRESBY'S RECIPE FOR PRESBYTERIANISM

If you take the water from the Baptists and the fire from the Methodists, you might generate enough steam to equal that of the Presbyterians.

PRESBYTERIANS GET A LITTLE TESTY WHEN

- ❑ the Catholics attending early Mass at the Church of Holy Activity across the street fill up our parking lot.
- ❑ the Property and Maintenance Committee redecorates the formal church parlors down to the marks on the furniture with the hope that no one will notice—and no one does.
- ❑ the bells of the Methodist Church down the street drown out the Christmas solo of the little boy in the Cherub Choir.
- ❑ they're stuck behind a truck that advertises G.O.D. (Guaranteed Overnight Delivery).
- ❑ some idiot makes up a list about Presbyterians getting testy.

WHISPERING HOPE

In spite of our serious demeanor, you will find that your fellow church members are a psychologically optimistic bunch, full of eager anticipation. Like the Roman god Janus, we look backward as well as forward to the future. And although we sometimes cast a sort of baleful eye at the rest of the world, we do plan ahead in church matters in a positive way.

For example, in towns so small that the Knights of Columbus and the Masons know one another's secrets, there's a First Presbyterian Church. Like in Bellflower, Missouri (pop. 403). That congregation went even further a few years back by appointing a new pastor who was over 70 years of age.

But there are First Presbyterian Churches in little towns all over the nation. The founders planned that someday they would help establish another Presbyterian church as the place grew. And in some cases, it worked.

You should look on all this warmly, while quoting something about hope springing eternal. It's a Presbyterian golden rule!

COUNT 'EM!

There are also a number of First Presbyterian Churches in big cities, and the older ones have staked out claims about their names. To make sure everybody knew of their national origin, some early settlers in Charleston, South Carolina, in 1731 named their gathering place the First (Scots) Presbyterian Church.

Another one, in Wilmington, Delaware, took no chances in the new world by calling itself the *First and Central* Church. And congregations in such diverse places as San Francisco and Huntington, New York have labeled themselves the *Old First* Presbyterian Church, presumably to preempt any newcomers who might call themselves the *New First* Presbyterian Church. And logic commands us to suppose that somewhere in the world there is the *Very First* Presbyterian Church.

Many congregations in the big towns have spawned other churches for so it was envisioned and thus the denomination has grown. So we have a Second Presbyterian Church in Louisville, Birmingham, and

Sioux City; a Third Presbyterian Church in Fort Wayne, Nebraska, Rockford, Illinois, Dubuque, Iowa and Rochester, New York. There's a Fourth Presbyterian Church in Knoxville, Tennessee with another in Chicago, the "Presbyterian City." And in Cincinnati there's a Seventh Presbyterian Church!

But don't worry. Today there are no Eighth Presbyterian Churches in the Presbyterian (U.S.A.) denomination, although it's probably not from a lack of optimistically trying. The ancient who said that he "would rather meet coming against me a whole regiment with drawn swords, than one Calvinist convinced that he is doing the will of God" probably understated the case. Or as King Charles I reportedly said, "There is nothing more dangerous than a Presbyterian fresh off his knees."

DOIN' IT!

Sometimes Presbyterian optimism and determination isn't enough. Witness this hoary old ditty reportedly inspired by the antics of an elder in a small town in Illinois. The last line is a major departure from the famous Edgar Guest poem.

Somebody said that it couldn't be done
But he with a chuckle replied,
That maybe it couldn't, but he would be one
Who wouldn't say so 'til he tried.
So he buckled right in with a trace of a grin on his face.
If he worried, he hid it.
He started to sing as he tackled the thing
That couldn't be done
—And he couldn't do it!

WHAT IT'S LIKE TO BE A PRESBYTERIAN!

Percy T. Presby on Long Island, New York tells this version of an old joke. A guy was walking across a bridge and saw a man ready to jump off.

He ran over to him and yelled "Stop, don't do it!"

The fellow said, "Why?"

"Well—because there is so much to live for!"

"Like what?"

"Well—ah, are you religious?"

"Yes."

"Me too! Are you Christian or Jewish?"

"Christian."

"Me too! Are you Catholic or Protestant?"

"Protestant."

"OK! Me too! Are you Baptist or Presbyterian?"

"Presbyterian."

"Fantastic! Me too! Are you a member of the Presbyterian Church in America or the Presbyterian Church (U.S.A.)?"

"Presbyterian Church (U.S.A.)"

"Yea! Me too! Are you in the Mid-Atlantic Synod or the Synod of the Northeast?"

"The Northeast."

"Wow, me too! Are you in the Presbytery of New York City or the Presbytery of Long Island?"

"Presbytery of New York City."

So the guy said, "Die, heretic" and pushed him off the bridge.

THE PRESBYTERIAN NATIONAL ANTHEM

Finally, the ultimate in many a Presbyterian's psyche is expressed most vividly in our unofficial national anthem. We've sung it at summer church camps, at retreats, and at worship services. It's in our hymnal and many choirs have a beautiful arrangement of it that is designed to lift the congregation right up off the pews!

It is, of course, "Kumbaya," which means—in an African language—"come by here." Everybody knows the melody, but few know the new words, written by Percy T. Presby in a fit of religious patriotism one night when he couldn't sleep.

So stand up now and sing this most joyful of Presbyterian songs, loudly and with good cheer. God will be listening!

The Presbyterian National Anthem (to the tune of "Kumbaya")

We're not Buddhists, Lord, no-sir-ree,
We're not Muslims, Lord, no-sir-ree
We're not Hindus, Lord, no-sir-ree
No, no-o, no-sir-ree.
We're not Baptists, Lord, no-sir-ree,
We're not Catholics, Lord, no-sir-ree,
We're not Lutherans, Lord, no-sir-ree,
No, no, Lord, no-sir-ree.

We're the Presbys, Lord, yes-sir-ree!
We're the Presbys, Lord, yes-sir-ree!
We're the Presbys, Lord, yes-sir-ree!

(Beeg Hollywood finish here!)
OH, LORD, YES-SIR-REEE!!!

About the Author

Bob Reed is a proud native of Marcus, Iowa (pop 1,171), who spent 25 years building and managing public television stations and as an executive at PBS. He has also served as a publisher and tenured professor and has penned dull, scholarly, research tomes including encyclopedias and dictionaries. This retiree is a Navy veteran and an awfully proud grandfather who plays that happiest of instruments—the banjo. But as his wife often reminds him, the difference between a banjo player and a treasury bond is that eventually the bond matures and makes money. He and his wife Max are members of the First Presbyterian Church of Northport (a harbor village on Long Island, New York) and sing in the Chancel Choir there—without the banjo.

Bob is neither an elder nor deacon in the church, for he paraphrases Groucho Marx in saying that he couldn't be a member of any topnotch group that would have him as a member. He reasons that feeling unworthy—far from disqualifying one for faith —is perhaps a requisite for having some.

Bob was raised a Methodist, and this little book grew out of his 13 years of continuing attempts to comprehend his new denomination. He is also the author of a collection of humorous short stories titled *The*

Potluck Dinner That Went Astray (Smyth and Helwys Publishing). And his next book is another collection of comic tales titled *The Choir That Couldn't Sing*. He thinks his very presence on this earth is proof that God has an unusual sense of humor. And he's certain that heaven is Iowa!

OTHER BOOKS BY BOB REED

Nonfiction

The American Telecommunications Market

Career Opportunities in Television, Cable, Video, and Multimedia

The Encyclopedia of Television, Cable, and Video

The Dictionary of Television, Cable, and Video

Fiction

The Potluck Dinner That Went Astray—And Other Tales of Christian Life

The Choir That Couldn't Sing (WIP)

"KEEP ONE!"
"GIVE ONE!"

THIS BOOK MAKES THE
PERFECT GIFT!

This little offering makes a grand gift for new members, or for your other colleagues in the denomination. Send it to someone as a little reminder that you cherish a Presbyterian friendship. Surprise and delight the church folks in your life. Share a smile and a bit of a giggle with them!

BRIGHTEN SOMEONE'S JOURNEY TODAY
GIVE THEM THE GIFT OF LAUGHTER!

The book is available through book stores or through
http://presby-book.net/
or from
Amazon.com, *Borders.com*, *BarnesandNoble.com*,
OR
iUniverse.com
or phone
1 (877) 823-9235

One for you and one for a friend...
IT'S A GREAT GIFT—ANYTIME!

OYEZ!
OYEZ!
OYEZ!

Percy T. Presby (Author Bob Reed)
is available for personal appearances at
Synod Meetings Presbytery Meetings
Seminars Retreats
Ordinations Installations
PW Luncheons Church Fairs
Annual Meetings
as well as at Weddings, Funerals, and Bar Mitzvahs!

In his period costume, Percy will regale the audience with 30 minutes of laugh-filled entertainment, based on his quips and sayings in this book. Begin—or spice up—your meeting with a mirthful session, complete with audience participation and a sing-along of Presby Songs!

FOR DETAILS, CONTACT
Reed-Gordon Books
285 Burr Road
East Northport, NY 11731
Phone/fax:631-462-5627
E-mail: *reedgordon@aol.com*

Printed in the United States
1040200003B/355-363

9 780595 152254